Practical Pre-School Books

Effective leadership and management in the EYFS

Contents

Introduction 2

Setting a vision and effective communication 5

Leadership style 7

Communication 9

Developing the team 19

Stages of team development 21

Motivation 24

Performance management 30

Target setting 33

Staff observation 35

Training 38

Monitoring children's progress and developing learning 49

Reflection on assessment and data collection 51

Working in partnership 58

Emotional barriers 58

Involving parents with play 61

Safeguarding 65

The manager and staff suitability 66

References 75

Acknowledgements 76

Published by Practical Pre-School Books, A Division of MA Education Ltd, St Jude's Church, Dulwich Road, Herne Hill, London, SE24 0PB.

Tel: 020 7738 5454 www.practicalpreschoolbooks.com

Design: Alison Coombes **fonthill**creative 01722 717043

All images taken by Lucie Carlier © MA Education Ltd.

ISBN 978-1-909280-89-2

Outstanding Early Years

Introduction

Leadership in early years is not an easy role. Often, individuals find themselves in the job with little training and support.

Leadership is very much about being pro-active, being seen to get on and get things done, making a difference, taking action. It is about how you are seen to lead your team, whilst keeping everything running and ensuring requirements are met.

This book is designed to unpick the role from a variety of perspectives, drawing together its many elements, including one of the hardest, the management of people. Each chapter explores a different aspect, beginning with leadership itself, moving through teamwork, performance management, monitoring, partnership working and safeguarding and welfare requirements. There is a wealth of reflective practice questions, task sheets and also staff meeting pointers in each chapter.

What is a leader and what is leadership?

A leader is someone who rises above the ordinary and helps their team decide what is important to achieve and accomplish. Leadership is about the ability to help your team define their goals and priorities and how to help them grow. A leader of a setting has to have a strong sense of intrinsic motivation and drive, desire and passion for both the job and the early years.

Leadership in early years, covers a broad remit and requires a complex mix of skills and knowledge. Everyday, your leadership is experienced and potentially questioned by staff and parents. Then one day every few years, it is judged by Ofsted.

The opposite chart looks at how Ofsted view early years leadership and management. This is then reflected and explored throughout the book.

The effectiveness of leadership and management of early years provision isn't just about the 'evidence', but, importantly, about the impression the leader/manager gives in relation to their skills, knowledge, passion and enthusiasm for their setting. How well they know their staff and the children, and how they are working to promote continuous improvement.

Outstanding grade descriptor

This table lists the grade descriptors for outstanding for leadership and management from the Inspection Handbook for Early Years (August 2015). The table unpicks each statement in the handbook, explaining what it means for you to then identify how you might develop practice in your setting.

Descriptor	What this means/evidence	Development in my setting
The pursuit of excellence in all the setting's activities is demonstrated by an uncompromising, highly successful drive to improve achievement or maintain the highest levels of achievement for all children.	This begins with your vision for the setting, how that is driven in conjunction with your staff team. How robust is your Quality Improvement Plan. What other forms of self evaluation are in place? Do you identify expected impact and actual impact, to track how improvements have made a difference? Do you have a Self Evaluation Form? If you are a multi room setting, are there development plans for individual rooms/units?	
Incisive evaluation of the impact of staff's practice leads to rigorous performance management, supervision and highly focused professional development. As a result, teaching is highly effective or improving rapidly.	Do you have a regular implemented cycle of supervision and appraisal? Is this documented with clear targets set and followed through? How often does the manager carry out observations on individual members of staff and rooms? How often do you model good practice. Are you supportive and do you challenge practice in order to improve? What opportunities do staff have to access professional development training, either outside the setting or internally, with an external trainer? How do you use information from staff observations and supervisions to inform continuous improvement targets for the setting as a whole?	
Leaders and managers actively seek, evaluate and act on the views of parents, staff and children to drive continual improvement.	How do you encourage and support reflection in the setting? How do you involve parents, staff and children in this process? Do you have a parent forum? Do you provide parent questionnaires? Do you ask the opinion of children about what they like in the setting? Do staff contribute to the Self Evaluation Form/ Quality Improvement Plan?	
Highly effective monitoring identifies where children may be slow to develop key skills so that specific programmes of support are implemented to help them catch up. Gaps in achievement between different groups of children, especially those for whom the setting receives additional funding are negligible or closing.	2 year old checks are completed and effective. Do you carry out effective cohort analysis to identify where children might be making less progress and identify and evaluate how to take action, to support increased progress? Do you look at comparison between different groups, children with SEND needs, children with EAL and those in receipt of EYPP funding? Do you track progress to identify if progress gaps are closing and link to identify how funding is spent and how this impacts on progress.	
The provider has excellent knowledge of the requirements of the Early Years Foundation Stage, and implements them highly effectively.	Are you up to date with and do you ensure that all the requires of the Statutory Framework are met? Staff are suitably qualified and ratios are maintained.	

Cont.

Outstanding grade descriptor

Leaders' deep understanding of the curriculum and how to apply it to meet the needs and interests of children results in all staff planning highly effective activities. As a result, children are exceptionally well prepared to move on, including, where appropriate, to school.	There are effective monitoring systems in place for the provision, ensuring that the children have a broad, balanced and appropriate experience in the setting. Staff are supported and encouraged in the activities and experiences they provide. Planning systems are flexible, responsive and effective for meeting the needs of the children. Learning journals/observations are monitored to promote quality and consistency. Regular summative assessments are carried out by staff. Strategies are in place to support children to become independent learners and are prepared for school. Links with feeder schools are established to support the transition process.	
Leaders set high standards for children's behaviour at all times. Exemplary relationships between staff provide an excellent model for children's behaviour towards each other.	Clear guidelines are set for the promotion of positive behaviour and policies and procedures are followed. Professional conduct and effective team work are supported and expectations are high, ensuring a positive atmosphere and modelled relationships. Staff behaviour policy.	
Highly effective partnership working leads to improvement in provision and outcomes for children and their families.	Partnership with parents is actively supported and parents are involved in the setting and encouraged to contribute observations and to learning journeys. Strategies are in place to support parents to be involved in the children's learning at home. Partnerships with other agencies are effective, particularly for children with additional needs. Community links are promoted to broaden the children's experiences and to support individual children.	
The promotion of equality, diversity and British values is at the heart of the setting's work. It is demonstrated through all its practices, including tackling any instances of discrimination and being alert to potential risks from radicalisation and extremisim.	This is evident and implicit in practice and staff are aware of their responsibilities in relation to the Prevent Duty and have clear understanding of British values.	
Safeguarding and welfare meet statutory requirements. Leaders and managers have created a culture of vigilance where children's welfare is actively promoted. Children are listened to and feel safe. Staff are trained to identify and support children who may be at risk of neglect or abuse and they report any concerns. Work with partner agencies to safeguard children's welfare is effective.	You have a single central record of staff information, qualifications and DBS checks. Staff are encouraged to sign up to the update service. All staff are up to date with First Aid and safeguarding training. The manager has undertaken designated person and safer recruitment training. All staff are aware of the whistle blowing policy and who to report to and this is displayed throughout the setting. All policies and risk assessments are up to date. Appropriate forms are completed with specific information for accidents, incidents, pre existing injuries and analysis undertaken as appropriate. Records of attendance and non attendance are recorded and flagged if necessary. Appropriate medication procedures are followed. Fire exits are signed, extinguishers serviced and regular fire drills undertaken.	

Setting a vision and effective communication

What do you need to do in order to be an effective leader? A leader needs to be a visionary and to have integrity, they need to inspire, be trusted and respected, have strong values and be consistent. Consistent in attitude, approach and mood. A leader is a role model and by the nature of their position sets the tone, atmosphere and culture of the setting. As a role model, the way they behave reflects their belief system and impacts on the behaviour of those they are leading.

Essentially, actions speak louder than words. An effective leader needs to be able to walk the walk and talk the talk. You need to demonstrate that your actions reflect your words. If you say you value the opinions and input of your team and then ignore that input, you are demonstrating a lack of respect and trust will be lost. The manager in a setting needs to demonstrate trust and respect for their team for it to be reciprocated. Trust and respect is a two-way process.

Leadership is about character, behaviour and relationships, being credible, open and honest, trusting, respecting, listening to and empowering your team. Having a focus on actions, development and improvement, being prepared to take risks and accept challenge. You need to be inquisitive, asking why? Why do we do that? Why do we do it that way? Can we make it better? How can we be the best we can possibly be? That inquisitiveness brings us back to the need to be a visionary, a visionary who inspires and motivates taking their team with them.

As a manager of a setting, you need a clear vision. This is about what you stand for, what you want the setting be and achieve, it is essentially an ethos or philosophy. The vision would also reflect the values of the setting. The vision can only be achieved with your team on board and working with you. Think of it like a train, you are the engine and the team are the carriages behind you. You want and need them to stay on the track behind you to reach the destination and not get derailed, go off on a branch line or get stuck at an earlier station. As the visionary leader in the setting, you will have an idea for your vision. However, this needs to be shared and discussed and not imposed. This means your team will have a sense of ownership of the vision and will work with you to achieve it.

The vision should be discussed at a staff meetings where thoughts and feedback are welcomed. You will need to explain your thoughts behind the vision and what it means and relates to in practice. Clear understanding of the vision is essential. Your team might have ideas and suggestions for modifications, often a different perspective can be illuminating.

The hard work then begins, how to implement the vision and maintain it in practice.

Begin by reflecting together on these key questions:

- What will the vision look like in practice?
- Where are we now in relation to the vision?
- Where do we want to get to/where would we like to be?
- How will we get there?
- How will we know we are getting there?
- How will we know we have achieved this?

The responses to these questions provide the basis that begins to form a plan of what you need to do and how. You may wish to do a SWOT analysis. This can help identify anything that might support or hinder the achievement of the vision. A SWOT analysis looks at:

- Strengths
- Weaknesses
- Opportunities
- Threats.

This kind of analysis can work well as a team building exercise and discussion and also gives everyone a deeper and broader understanding of the organisation as a whole. It therefore then feeds into the sense of ownership, bringing about a sense of the team working together, to build on strengths, tackle weaknesses, strategise against threats and exploit opportunities.

Strengths	Weaknesses
■ Consistent staff team ■ Outdoor area ■ Partnership with parent.	■ No access to CPD training ■ Lack of provision for maths area of learning and development ■ Inconsistency in learning journals.
Opportunities	**Threats**
■ New housing development ■ Fundraising publicity.	■ 30 hour funding ■ Schools taking in younger children.

The above is an example of the type of issues that might be identified. You might want to do a separate SWOT analysis from a management perspective too.

Once all this information from the vision discussion and SWOT has been collated, you can then feed this into a Quality Improvement Plan. The QIP may also include targets identified through supervision and appraisals (See Chapter 3). There is a proforma for the QIP on page 17.

The targets on your QIP need to be **SMART**:

Specific: clear, concise, definite and understood by everyone.

Measurable: to track progress and be able to quantify the success.

Agreed: with everyone concerned.

Realistic: achievable, if challenging.

Time bound: a date by which the target needs to be achieved.

When you write up your QIP, it can be helpful to break down each target into component parts, so it is clear how it is anticipated it will be achieved. You should also identify who will have responsibility for ensuring each target is achieved. Finally, you should identify what you think the expected impact of this improvement will be on the children, the setting, staff and parents depending on the nature of the target. Once the target has been achieved and had time to embed, you revisit the target and identify what the actual impact was in comparison to what you identified as the expected impact. This enables you to measure the success and adapt or develop it if necessary.

When writing your QIP, you should identify how often it will be reviewed and updated and progress tracked. You may wish to have a QIP for the whole setting or break it down into areas linked with inspection criteria. A QIP is a working document and all staff should be aware of what is included as everyone will be playing a part in the achievement of the targets. The review of the QIP and progress can be reflected upon with these questions:

- What are we on track to achieve?
- What are we doing well?
- What is working?
- What should we be doing more of?
- What have we learnt so far?
- What are we not doing so well, in relation to meeting targets and why?
- What should we be doing differently?
- Should we be putting more resources into achieving a particular target?
- Do we need to adjust any of our targets?
- Are there any factors hindering progress?

The Quality Improvement Plan is a key part in demonstrating your commitment to continuous improvement. It isn't about everything in your setting being perfect, but about recognising what you want to improve and develop and demonstrating how it will be done.

Obviously, once completed it is important that what you have said will happen, actually happens. You as the manager have specific targets as well as your team. You need to lead by example, demonstrating that you are meeting your targets, so your team work towards that as well. Prior to everyone working on the QIP targets, you need to ensure that all concerned are clear about the objectives, what they are trying to achieve, how that will happen and that you will be available if they need to ask questions.

Leadership style

Everything that happens in the setting, or doesn't happen, is influenced by your style of leadership. There are three key styles of leadership, but before we explore those, let us consider organisational structure and authority.

As the leader, you have authority. Authority is about your right to guide and direct the actions of others and encourage and support them to attain the goals you set. You also have key responsibility, this is the obligation you have and that you place on others to carry out a task or specific role.

Finally, accountability, you are accountable to your employer (if applicable) or committee and to each member of your team.

Organisational structure

The organisation structure is the system of arrangements between the various positions members of staff hold.

The structure of how an organisation is established is explained in the table below.

concerned with	involves	seen in
■ how the work of an organisation is divided and assigned to individuals, groups and departments ■ how the required co-ordination is achieved.	■ allocating tasks and responsibilities to individuals e.g. how much choice they have about how they work ■ specifying and defining jobs ■ designing the formal reporting relationships ■ deciding on the number of levels in the hierarchy ■ deciding on the span of control of each supervisor and manager.	■ organisation chart, job descriptions, establishing boards, committees and working parties ■ rules, policies and procedures ■ hierarchy ■ goal clarification ■ temporary task forces ■ permanent project teams ■ liaison roles ■ integrator roles.

Clear organisational structure, means that reporting lines are clear and responsibilities are allocated effectively. It brings a sense of order and stability to the setting. It is also particularly helpful for new staff in terms of getting an understanding of the setting.

How everything flows and the general effectiveness is down to you and how you lead the team, your style of leadership and ability to communicate effectively.

Everyone has a leadership style they feel comfortable with, what we must realise is that there are different styles of leadership that are required for different situations, and we may have to switch to a different style of leadership to get the job accomplished. Different teams and individuals will respond to different styles of leadership. The effective leader can match the style effectively and this is therefore reflective of how well you know your staff.

Autocratic style

Characteristics:

- tells others what to do
- limits discussion on new ideas and new ways of doing things
- group does not experience feeling of teamwork.

When effective:

- time is limited
- individuals/group lack skill and knowledge
- group does not know each other
- inexperienced staff who need more guidance
- staff lack of confidence
- you need to challenge practice
- when important action needs to be taken, e.g. relating to safeguarding
- evacuating the building

When ineffective

- developing a strong sense of team is the goal
- some degree of skill/knowledge is in members
- group wants an element of spontaneity in their work.

Democratic style

Characteristics:

- involves group members in planning and carrying out activities
- asks before telling
- promotes the sense of teamwork.

When effective:

- time is available
- group is motivated and/or a sense of team exists
- some degree of skill or knowledge among members of the group
- staff have good use of initiative
- you want to encourage a team to develop an area of provision and welcome ideas and suggestions
- you want to delegate and give others responsibility.

When ineffective:

- group is unmotivated
- no skill/knowledge is in members
- high degree of conflict present.

Laissez Faire style

Characteristics:

- gives little or no direction to group/individuals
- opinion is offered only when requested
- a person does not seem to be in charge.

When effective:

- high degree of skill and motivation
- routine is familiar to participants
- experienced and effective team who work well together
- strong use of initiative.

When ineffective:

- low sense of team/interdependence
- low degree of skill/knowledge is in members
- group expects to be told what to do.

The ability to flit between the styles takes confidence and knowledge and isn't about being inconsistent, but carefully judging each situation and individual and identifying how to get the best of it or them, what will work. The majority of the time, you will adopt the democratic style of leadership as this is the most effective for the majority of the time. However, if that becomes permanent, it means that your leadership is becoming ineffective as there are times when it will not work and is inappropriate.

Communication

The use of different leadership styles, is closely linked with communication and effective communication skills and strategies. Communication is a two-way process and is about sharing ideas, thoughts and suggestions. It is about expressing feelings and concerns and is about discussion. Non-verbal communication is as important as verbal communication and can be helpful in reading reactions and responding. In fact, when you break communication down it looks like this:

- 7% content
- 38% your voice
- 55% body language.

It isn't so much what you say, but how you say it. Effective communication gets results and people feel involved and informed, ineffective communication means tasks don't get done and generally there is a lack of commitment.

When we communicate there are important steps and considerations to remember, to ensure we get across what needs to be said and understood. Equally, it is important to think about how we respond to others when we are in the position of listening.

If you are delivering the communication you are the sender, if you are listening you are the receiver, here are some key points to consider and remember about sending and receiving:

The checklist for the sender

Do:

- be clear about what you want to say, get to the point
- look at the person you are speaking to, this helps engage them
- speak clearly, matching the language you use to the receiver, anticipating how they might react and respond
- consider the feelings of the person you are speaking to, are they likely to be upset, happy, confused, cross, how can you help them?
- choose carefully the time and place you speak, minimise distractions
- check that the person has understood what you have said, ask them if it's all clear and makes sense, do they understand what they need to do?
- make sure your words match up with the way you are sounding
- vary the tone and pace at which you speak so that your voice is interesting to listen to and therefore more engaging.

Don't:

- complicate what you are saying with too much detail or difficult language, avoid jargon and acronyms
- talk so much that the other person has no chance to comment or ask questions, but give opportunity for response and queries, this will aid understanding
- be vague, but give concrete examples, this helps to illustrate a point and bring about clearer understanding and awareness
- put down, attack or ridicule the person you are talking to
- use particular ideas you know will irritate the other person
- ignore signs of confusion, resentment or disinterest in the person to whom you are speaking, this means you have lost them, respond to these signs by pausing giving them a chance to speak
- speak in a detached, remote fashion, to keep the listener engaged you need to remain engaged
- pretend or exaggerate, keep to the facts.

The checklist for the receiver

Do:

- look at the person who is speaking to you and give them your full attention, this shows them you are listening and interested
- recognise how the speaker feels about what they are saying, if appropriate show empathy and sympathy
- look for points to agree with rather than to argue with, this is important for your response and it demonstrates you have been listening
- give a quick summary of what you have heard, this enables you to reflect on your response whilst ensuring you have heard and understood correctly.

Don't:

- interrupt the speaker to give your views, let them get to the end of what they need to say and then they will be better positioned to listen to your response and in some instances in a calmer manner
- let your previous experience of the person put you off, treat each conversation as a new experience
- let prejudices get in the way of listening to what has been said, don't make assumptions or jump to conclusions before someone has spoken
- be negative about or belittle what the person is saying, it might seem trivial to you but to the speaker it is important
- change the subject, remain focused
- fidget or distract the speaker.

As you prepare and plan what you wish to convey, it can be helpful to think about these 6 steps, especially if you are nervous:

The 6 steps of communication

1. **know your purpose,** what is it you need to get across, what do you want to achieve by the end of the communication?

2. **decide the best method**, verbal face to face, on the phone or in writing?

3. **overcome barriers,** don't let nerves of previous bad experiences put you off, if there are practical barriers e.g. language, identify strategies to help.

4. **transmit the message,** remembering the guidance for the sender.

5. **give time for message to be understood,** give time for reflection and processing and enable questions for clarity.

6. **obtain feedback,** follow up, was everything understood and was there a follow through.

In an early years setting, we communicate in a variety of ways and the broader the strategies and methods we use, the more likely we are to ensure everyone feels informed and involved.

Communication strategies

How many of these do you do and are there any you could introduce?

- Briefings (morning and/or evening)
- Staff newsletter emailed weekly, fortnightly or monthly
- Monthly staff meetings with agenda distributed before and minutes emailed after and available as hard copy in the setting
- Leadership meetings, room meetings
- Communication whiteboard in office/rooms/staff rooms
- Whatsapp group
- Closed Facebook group
- Professional development/training sessions together
- Supervision meetings
- One to one meetings
- Open door policy, chatting
- Staff notice board.

The broader and wider the range of communication within a setting, the more likely you are to ensure everyone feels informed.

What we choose to communicate is just as important as how we communicate. We need to use communication as a tool to support effective leadership. The ability to communicate and articulate runs through all the different aspects of leadership.

Often, ineffective communication can cause frustration and irritation, we think we have communicated one thing or we make assumptions based on what we have said and the understanding associated, only for a different outcome to occur.

The need for clarity is essential and removes any possibility of ambiguity. You need to be clear and specific with staff to ensure there is no misunderstanding. It is always helpful to start with the yes, what you can do, what you do want to happen and what you would like to happen and then work your way back to the 'no' if that applies. You want your staff team to focus on the positives and what they can do, how they can do something and what they need to do. If this is approached with clear knowledge and understanding; communication is effective and positive.

You do not want a punitive culture where a team become fearful of what a manager is going to say, with the focus on what they are not allowed to do.

Communication realities

This table gives examples of what we may say to practitioners, what we think will happen, how they actually respond and how we can change our communication to get the result we desired.

You ask	What you think will happen	What actually happens	How to change
You ask a member of staff to go into another room for the day to cover.	You assume the staff member will be happy to do this and go happily into the room.	The member of staff is unhappy and resents being asked to go into another room. They go into the room in a bad mood, and add little to the room.	Explain why it is needed. That you will move them back if you can later in the day. Give them a specific focus for that day in the room, this could be to do with developing an aspect of provision or observing a particular child. Discuss in a staff meeting to ensure all staff are aware of the why this is sometimes necessary. Keep a record/rota, so you are not always asking the same staff to cover.
You ask a member of staff to set up the outside area.	The member of staff will immediately go outside and set up ready for the children.	The member of staff decides to leave setting up until their group of children are ready to go outside.	Put in place a clear rota, for areas or perhaps room based. Give a practitioner overall responsibility for the outdoor provision. Monitor to ensure planning takes place for the outside.
You need to make sure your observations up to date.	They will go and check their learning journals and ensure their observations are up to date.	They forget, unsure what you mean by up to date. Think their observations are fine.	Be clear about what you mean by up to date.
Can you make your observations longer.	From their next observation, they will make them longer and more detailed.	They don't change their observations as they are unsure what you meant or make them longer by including unnecessary detail.	Go through observations with the member of staff explaining what you mean by needing to make them longer, show an example. Ask them to go away and do an observation and check back with you later that day.
You ask a member of staff to change a display.	They will immediately go and begin to work on the display to get it done quickly.	Several days later the display has not been changed.	Give timescale, say exactly when you want it done.
You ask the staff to eat with the children.	The member of staff will sit with their plate on the table and model good table manners with the children.	They are sitting back, plate on lap, just using a fork, but telling the children to use a knife and a fork.	Set clear guidelines for adult role modelling at meal times, specify your expectations.
you say	**what they hear**	**what actually happens**	**how to change**
We need to make sure there is more variety with cooking activities, balance sweet and savoury, not just cakes.	We can't make cakes with the children anymore.	Cooking activities decrease.	Ensure you explain why there needs to be a balance, challenge staff to find recipes using unusual ingredients or give some suggestions.
Can you make sure your room tidy is at the end of the day.	That their room needs to be tidy.	The room is given a cursory tidy up.	Set clear expectations regarding what you mean by clean and tidy at the end of the day, so that the room is ready for the next day.
Why were you late?	You asking them why but no emphasis on the need to be punctual.	They continue to be late on occasions.	Lateness needs to be effectively challenged and clear emphasis on the impact on everyone and that lateness will not be tolerated, only in very exceptional circumstances.

You need to facilitate and enable the use of initiative within the setting. A culture and feel where there is no ambiguity and staff feel empowered is more likely to encourage initiative and innovation. Essentially, a manager uses their personality to lead by example and therefore stimulate a particular culture. If the manager is perceived to make things better and welcoming of innovation and ideas, team morale and productivity will be increased.

Effective communication is a key element in this process of facilitating initiative.

Communication can be looked at from three different perspectives:

As perception
Individuals can have a different understanding or perception of communication, so we need to ensure we communicate in a manner that is easy to understand, remembering that sometimes you need to be explicit and state the obvious to avoid assumptions being made.

As expectation
We have a tendency to hear what we want to hear and we learn to expect certain communications in certain situations. As a consequence, confusion often occurs when these expectations are not met, so when we want people to take notice of anything new or different we wish to communicate, we need to highlight it so they will take notice and be clear in explaining our expectation of their response and actions.

Making demands
Communication makes demands on both the person delivering the communication and the person listening. The sender needs to ensure that they communicate in an effective and easily understood manner. You have to remember that the listener may choose not to listen and will switch off, if the message is delivered in a manner which is not easily understood, perhaps using too much jargon or at an inconvenient time.

If you look at communication from the perspective of your staff team, it can help ensure that you are communicating what they need to know:

- A clear understanding of their role and responsibilities
- What is expected of them in relation to standards and quality
- Their legal obligations
- How they are doing, individually, with their team and in the setting as a whole
- That their contribution is valued and recognized
- They are kept up to date on plans and developments
- They will be consulted on decisions that personally affect them.

Something that is crucial to communicate and to reiterate, is your expectations you have of your team. Yes, they have a job description and an outline of roles and responsibilities, but expectation is about making the specifics clear. It can be helpful to begin with a staff meeting discussion asking your team what they think your expectations of them are, that is a broad question. However, getting their viewpoint can be revealing and interesting and gives an insight into what they consider important and a reflection on the messages you have given them. This can also be used as an opportunity to explain why you expect something of them. Explanations can bring about deeper understanding and therefore, a greater likelihood that those expectations will be met.

Examples of expectations

- To form attachments with their key children and support their individual needs and maintain their learning journal
- Immediate and correct completion of accident forms (a legal requirement which provides evidence if a child is later discovered to have an additional injury)
- Completion of the register as each child arrives (a legal requirement and necessary for logging who is in the building at any one time)
- Support children to be as independent as development allows at lunch time (link to PSED, Physical development and British values)
- To return to their room on time after lunch (to ensure ratios are maintained and to ensure everyone is able to have a break)
- Attend staff meetings (to be with the team, discuss issues, be informed and up to date, part of their professional development).

As well as highlighting your expectations of your team it can also be beneficial to ask them what they expect of you. This can help you to see how they view you and explain what might or might not be realistic in relation to their expectations. As well as the open discussion, you might like to undertake a 360 review.

360 review

You might have an idea of how you are as a leader in your setting or organisation and you may be appraised by a line manager, ultimately though, it is the staff you lead who perhaps know best. Asking them how they see you and what they think of your leadership skills, whilst perhaps scary and daunting can be informative and revealing.

A 360 review promotes open discussion and communication and demonstrates to your team not only that you trust and respect them, but that you also value their views and opinions. It can be very simple, with just a few questions, which are open ended and meaningful. Through them you are simply asking 'how am I as a leader?'

Example questions
In what ways have I improved the setting in the past year?
How have I supported you in your work in the setting?
What do you think are my strengths?
Identify something you feel I could do better in the setting.
How effective do you think I am at solving problems?
Can you give examples of how I have motivated the team this year?

Once the questions have been asked and responses received, you need to collate and identify what the responses tell you and any actions and developments necessary. It is essential then, that your conclusions are shared with your staff team.

This chapter has only begun to scratch the surface of the role of the early years manager, so before continuing, some focus on time management seems appropriate. As a manager, time is precious and there never seems to be enough hours in the day to fit everything in. Reflecting on these time management questions can be helpful:

- Why does your job exist? What is the prime purpose of your job role?
- What are your priorities and why? The why is important and linked to the above question, as it can help identify what your top priorities are
- How do you currently use your time? This can be a tricky question to answer as no two days will be the same. It can help to keep a log over, say, a fortnight, to analyse exactly where your time goes and then how that can be better balanced.
  - How much time did I spend on the really important tasks that help the setting grow and improve? This includes staff development
  - Am I playing to my strengths?
  - What am I doing that I could delegate? (delegation is discussed in Chapter 3)
  - Are staff coming to me with the same problems and issues over and over again? Why, is there a training need? Are they using this as a get out the room excuse? Are they asking me questions that I don't need to answer? Do I need to make clearer the reporting lines and who has control of certain elements of the job?
  - Should I be saying 'now' and 'not now' more often when faced with interruptions? How much do I interrupt other people?
  - What am I going to do to eliminate time wasting?
- Could I allocate certain times in the week for office work, where at these times everyone knows I am not to be interrupted? This golden time can prove productive. Allocate certain regular tasks e.g. rotas to a certain day of the week
- Produce a regular 'to do' list and put times in priority order and identify what can be delegated
- If it is important do it now, especially if it is a task you do not enjoy
- Break difficult tasks down into smaller achievable tasks.

The benefit of effective time management can be great to allow:

- A sense of empowerment and control of what you need to achieve
- More effective use of your time
- Increased staff motivation, through additional responsibility and giving a clear framework to how your time is used
- Problem solving and decision making
- Clearer priorities and achievement of tasks
- For those to whom you delegate, a clearer understanding of your role and responsibilities, which means they will be better able to handle things in your absence.

The effective manager/leader in an early years setting is reflective, proactive and supportive of their team, additionally though, it is essential they give themselves space. Space to do, reflect and get on without interruption, even if it is only 20 minutes everyday, invest in that precious time and you will ultimately be investing in the setting and your team.

To summarise, these basic principles will help you establish authority and gain trust and respect, therefore be effective as a leader.

- Always be fair and consistent in your approach and treatment of staff and situations
- Ensure you communicate effectively both verbally and non-verbally and keep people informed and up to date
- If possible, involve all team members in decisions and policy reviews
- Ensure you are up to date with and understand all administrative procedures
- Be positive and enthusiastic
- Ensure you give recognition for a job well done
- Be seen to be proactive and get things done
- Don't put off unpleasant tasks
- Accept responsibility for mistakes
- Show trust and respect towards others
- Don't let the job make you or others miserable and unhappy.

Step by step assertiveness

This is a guide to the process of being assertive in certain situations.

1. Identify what you actually want to accomplish, your goal for being assertive, e.g. parent to pay fees on time.

2. Clarify how being assertive will help you achieve this.

3. Analyse what you would usually do to avoid being assertive in a situation or with a particular person.

4. Clarify what the likely advantages of being assertive instead would be. The direct expression of your

Case study Setting a Vision

In November 2011, Ofsted inspected and declared our setting to be 'Inadequate'. this was primarily due to an error in the Safeguarding policy, but also a lack of parental involvement in children's learning, as well as inadequate self-evaluation.

Following the inspection, the Manager resigned with immediate effect and unfortunately did not return to the setting. Although I was approached initially to take over the Manager's role, I declined as I did not feel ready for the responsibility and would have felt out of my depth. However, it became increasingly obvious that we had very little time before the next inspection and improvements were required immediately. As I already knew the families, policies, procedures and staff, I decided that I would take on the role of Manager for a temporary period until the next inspection.

The period which followed was incredibly difficult, even though support from parents during this difficult time was tremendous. I experienced a feeling of being completely overwhelmed with the task ahead of me with no experience of managing a setting and a huge lack of faith in my own abilities. The first task was to come together as a team, looking forward to the future by setting a vision and the goals to be achieved. Obviously, the vision was for us to return to being a 'Good' setting in the eyes of Ofsted as we felt we owed this to the parents and children. We didn't want parents to be embarrassed about sending their children to Busy Bees or be worried about the quality of learning and development. This led on to a vision of developing a setting where parents were completely involved and engaged in their child's learning. I began by ensuring that all parents were aware of the role of the Key Person so they understood their responsibilities and how they were an advocate for their child. A greater awareness of the role, I felt, would develop and strengthen the relationship between parent and key person, so it could be more effective and trusting.

Although Learning Journeys were already completed for all children, these were not shared regularly with parents, which needed to change in order to improve outcomes for children. The Key Persons effectively engaged with parents, encouraging them to take the Learning Journey home, look through it with the child and add their own photos and comments. This really helped us build a clearer picture of the child, allowing us to support their interests and development more effectively in the setting.

Communication was key to developing our vision for the future. I acknowledged that a method of communication which was preferred by one parent, may not be the best form for another. It was important to us to offer as many different forms of communication as possible in order to engage parents and share information about the children's time with us. I began to update the website regularly with news and photos and in time I set up a Facebook page and Twitter account to increase our communication outlets. Texts and emails were used, as were display boards, letters and newsletters alongside our already excellent verbal exchanges.

The months following the 'Inadequate' inspection saw us really evaluate the purpose of Busy Bees, resulting in us celebrating the child and their own ability to lead the learning. The previous method of planning was scrapped in favour of a more child lèd approach which was developed by tuning into the children's interests. Children were more engaged in activities on offer, needs and wishes will minimise misinterpretation and misunderstanding of your requirements and maximise the probability of the parent responding to your request to pay the fees on time, for example.

5. Identify what might prevent you from being assertive. Are you holding false notions about the consequences of being assertive? Could it be that your non-assertive approach is related to mistaken beliefs about the need for politeness in interactions about money? Do you fear an aggressive or tearful response from the parent?

6. Identify any other sources of anxiety and think of how you will cope with and reduce them. Are you anxious about what the parent might say about you to the staff or other parents? Think about and reaffirm your own rights in the situation.

7. Construct a model response that you would feel comfortable saying in the situation or to the person and practise it aloud several times, redefine if necessary until you find one that feels comfortable.

8. When the situation arises, have the courage to put into practice your assertive response knowing that you will probably have another opportunity to try again.

9. Reflect upon the results of your assertive statement in terms of what you liked about what you did, and the outcome, and what you would change next time.

improving learning and development. As we became more tuned in, there was a realisation that our structured snack time at 10am everyday was not working. Children's play was interrupted for them to sit down together to eat snack, even if they weren't hungry. This inhibited the uninterrupted opportunities for play, impacting on the vision for the setting and children. I made the decision to introduce a café style snack where children could join the table when ready. Children needed the opportunity to develop independence during this time so were encouraged to serve themselves under supervision from a member of staff. After eating, they put their plates in the washing up bowl before returning to their play. Following the introduction of the café style snack, children were observed to be more engaged in their play and interactions and a natural break in this would result in them joining the table for snack. This put the emphasis on the child deciding when they were hungry and thirsty or just ready for social time at the snack table.

Once the above changes had been implemented, as well as our safeguarding policy being updated, confidence amongst the team grew. Although we knew it would be difficult to go straight from Inadequate to Good, we were going to give it a very good shot! In July 2012, we were resinspected and judged to be 'Good'. The day went incredibly well and we were delighted to be told by the inspector that she would have liked to have judged us as Outstanding, but unfortunately, we needed to show that the changes were sustainable over time.

Now that the inspection had taken place, I was due to step down, having agreed to manage for a temporary period only. However, I eventually decided to continue as a Manager of Busy Bees, which was also an opportunity for me to put into practice the knowledge I was gaining through attending University to study for my Foundation Degree in Early Years.

Even though the pressure of an inspection had eased, the vision of Busy Bees continued to flourish. Provision was evaluated, highlighting areas for improvement so we could provide an environment in which children would thrive. In 2014, I introduced an online Learning Journey system which has dramatically increased parental engagement in their child's time at Busy Bees. Investments were made in staff training including Forest School, phonics, safeguarding, SENCO and Team Leading which impacted on the practice with the children.

I wanted learning to be extended outside of the setting, so I planned opportunities for us to be more active within the community. We became more involved with our local 'In Bloom' organisation and achieved a silver award for this. Visits out became a regular occurrence with children having time to play at the park, walk into town for traffic surveys or to look at patterns, borrow books from the library and see the advent displays in church.

Our next inspection at Busy Bees was in April 2016 and we were delighted to be graded as 'Outstanding' in all areas. It was a very positive experience and I finally felt that I had accomplished something in collaboration with the wonderful staff team, children, parents and the community. Parents can feel proud for their child to attend Busy Bees. Our vision now is stronger than ever as we have confidence in what we can achieve for the children in our care.

Emma Davis, Busy Bees @ LPS Ledbury, Herefordshire

How to be a listener

To listen properly you have to be able to hear what isn't being said and consider non-verbal clues transmitted through body language.

- **Focus**
  First of all focus, focus on not talking while the person speaking. Don't interrupt however tempting it might be, wait. If you interrupt you will cut off the speakers' flow and a vital piece of information might get lost. When the person speaking has finished talking you may need to clarify to ensure you have understood their message correctly.

- **Respond non-verbally**
  Give reassurance and indicate you are listening to the speaker by nodding or using other gestures to encourage them to continue. Maintain eye contact but don't stare – show them you are listening and understand what is being said.

- **Don't be distracted**
  Don't let yourself be distracted by doodling, shuffle papers, looking out of the window, playing with a pen or a paperclip etc. If you are engaged in these distracting activities, not only will you not be focused, they will become a distraction and irritant to the speaker.

- **Be understanding**
  Try to understand the other person's point of view. Try to look at issues from their perspective, by having an open mind we can more fully empathise with the speaker. If the speaker says something that you disagree with, then wait until they have finished before you express your view and opinion.

- **Wait**
  A pause, even a long pause, does not necessarily mean that the speaker has finished. Be patient and let the speaker continue in their own time, sometimes it takes time to formulate what to say and how to say it. Never interrupt or finish a sentence for someone. Remember everyone has a different way of speaking - some people are for more nervous or shy than others, some people like to pace whilst talking - others like to sit still. Focus on what is being said and try to ignore everything else.

- **Listen to the expression in the voice**
  Volume and tone tell us a lot about how someone feels about what they are saying. Tune in as these can help you to understand the feeling behind what is being said.

Staff meeting discussion points

These are suggestions of points to discuss in staff meetings which are supportive of developing practice.

- Expectations
  - What you expect of the staff
  - What they expect of you
  - What they expect of each other
- What does being a professional mean?
- Give them examples of situations that you as the manager have to resolve, e.g. two staff phone in sick, you need to maintain ratios, what would they do?

This is about helping them to see the implications of their actions, insight into the manager's role understanding of legal requirements.

Quality improvement plan (QIP)

Action and reason	Process	By whom	By when	Expected impact	Actual impact

Vision

Reflect on your vision for your setting, by completing this table.

What is your VISION?	Do your team know your vision? How do you know they know?	Do they have ownership over the vision? If yes, how has this been established and maintained?	Is it being implemented? What needs to be done?

Case study Beach school leadership

Cassie Holland, a beach school leader, describes her leadership challenges and how it is monitored.

I lead beach school once a week for half a day for two nurseries in Bristol. We take the pre-school children and operate on a 1:4 ratio. The children have an amazing time, paddling, splashing, throwing pebbles of different sizes into the sea, beach art with what we find e.g. driftwood, shells, sea weed, they climb on rocks, make marks, find crabs, go onto the grass with magnifiers, make marks. We have even done yoga on the beach. What we do changes according to the children's interests, the season and the tide.

The expectation is for all staff to be fully involved, no matter how messy on the mud flats. We outline in interview now that beach school is an integral part of pre-school life and what will be expected. It had to become part of the recruitment process, to emphasise the importance and expectations.

Beach school is a different kind of interaction with the children, you have nothing to hide behind. We take limited resources and use what we find, there is no routine and it can be threatening. It's more about responding to children's thoughts and interests there and then. This can be incredibly daunting.

During induction, we go through the importance of beach school, the operating procedures and health and safety. There is an introduction to theories to back up we interact and teach e.g. zone of proximal development. We discuss recognising teachable moments, having to respond, using skills and sustained shared thinking. It has been a challenge but worthwhile.

We provide all-in-one water proof clothes for staff so they have no reason not to get messy. They are kept at the nursery and washed there too. Everyone is also provided with wellies. It is about removing barriers and issues, taking away excuses; so full involvement is easier. We are supporting staff to meet the expectations of them and I try to predict what issues might lie ahead and prepare.

We take around 24 children each time and travel to the beach by train, we found that, often, the journey time was an unfocused time, so we introduced planning cards for the train, to enable the thinking process and to make the journey more meaningful. We sit in groups on the train and talk about what happened the week before and use photo prompts, thinking about what they might like to do this week.

Each session has a reflective question for staff which they feedback on and discuss together. On return to nursery, the children do reflective beach school floor books.

One of the consequences of beach school has been a greater involvement in the local community. When we walk to the station we walk down Cotham Hill, where there are lots of shops, and people come out and wave to us, and comment on us being on our way to beach school. We are now working with Severnside Community Rail Partnership to water plants at the station as part of a volunteering project. There are herbs planted at the station as part of the edible Bristol project, so people can come and take some leaves to use. We are also involved in planting at the station as well!

Cassie Holland, Archfield House Day Nursery, Bristol.

Developing the team

To deliver effective early years provision, a leader is reliant on their staff. They need to build, develop and nurture their staff to bring out the best in the individuals and therefore the team, ensuring cohesion and delivery of high quality provision. Sometimes you inherit a team, sometimes you get to build your own, but one certainty is that the team will constantly develop, change and evolve. Within the setting there might be more than one, the overall staff team and then smaller teams in different rooms or classrooms.

Important things to consider when building and developing a team

Having a shared understanding of the aims and policies of early years education
This is about a common framework under which everyone works, formed by policies and the statutory framework, as well as the individual vision and ethos of the setting. It helps to clarify and set what everyone is striving to achieve.

Having a shared sense of purpose
This is about the team working together to benefit the children e.g. following a routine, rotas or how a particular child's behavior is managed.

Having good working relationships based on trust and respect
This is essential between all team members as it enables effective working practices. Trust and respect have to be earnt and these are established in a variety of ways, e.g. being consistent, doing your job well, being supportive of others.

Having a good leader/co-ordinator to manage early years provision
A team needs to be nurtured, guided and developed, to bring out the best in the individual and in the setting/school.

Having a clear understanding of roles and responsibilities
A team is a bit like a jigsaw puzzle, and everyone needs to know where everyone else fits, so they can be clear about their role and place.

Having skills and strategies for effective communication
Everyone needs to be kept informed and aware of changes, a mix of strategies is necessary. Equally, though, individuals need to ensure they keep themselves informed.

Having team members who are adaptable and flexible in their approach
For a team to work effectively, members need to be supportive of each other and therefore flexible in their responses and approach, this is also a necessity based on the unpredictability of children.

Managing time
So that all the above can take place, this is particularly important when there are adults working part-time, whose need for involvement is no different from those adults who work full-time. This is about leadership approach to keeping everyone informed and up to date and feeling included.

The success of any team is dependent on members feeling involved and mutually respected, being given recognition, responsibility and the opportunity to share experience and expertise.

Maslow's hierarchy of needs and motivation

How can this be achieved?

- **Feeling involved and welcome:** through an effective induction, clearly defined roles, meetings, having specific responsibilities, having a voice, being listened to, and asked for ideas and contributions
- **Mutually respected:** with contributions valued, individuality and unique skills recognised, professional boundaries clear and individuals trusted
- **Given recognition:** achievements shared in newsletters with parents and colleagues, praise and acknowledgment to be included, verbal positives and responsibilities given
- **Responsibility:** promotion of skills and strengths, taking lead with new initiatives, delegation and ways of supporting others
- **Opportunity to share experience and expertise:** cascade from training, delivering sessions in staff meetings, running workshops, through supervision and supporting others.

All of this takes time to work through and build and needs effective leadership, supported by clear communication. We need to understand the process and structure to be effective in developing and building a team. Team building is the process of helping the team to improve its performance by helping members to understand their own roles. Team work is fundamental to organisational performance and team performance is central to organisational effectiveness. So what that means is, we need team work for a setting to perform well and to be effective.

Neugebauer (1984) has devised a specific framework for team building in early childhood settings which has five steps:

1. Set achievable goals which have been mutually agreed upon by members of the team.
2. Clarify roles, team members work most effectively when their roles are clear to all and free of conflict. Each team member should be aware of who is responsible for what. The leader needs to analyse the group to make sure that someone is taking responsibility for team task roles, and team maintenance.
3. Build supportive relationships, build in opportunities for feedback, develop trust and provide resources to stimulate a co-operative team spirit.
4. Encourage active participation which capitalises on the knowledge and skills of individual team members. In an atmosphere of acceptance, team members will be encouraged to contribute their ideas, opinions and energies.

Case study Being a new manager in an established setting

Rebecca Pickles of BCOT Day Nursery describes her experience as an experienced manager starting at a new nursery.

When I first started I could see there was a need for change and development both within the provision and in practice. I began by having one to one meetings with each member of staff to help me get to know them and to get their thoughts about the nursery and what they thought might be the areas for improvement.

This was all supported by observations in rooms and by spending time working in the rooms. I needed to be sure whether what I observed was a one off or an ongoing issue.

I felt it was important to wait and take my time before implementing change. I waited until I felt the staff were more comfortable with me, had got to know me and I had got to know them, so trust and respect had been established. I felt they would then be more likely to work with me and be more open to change and developing and improving practice.

Rebecca Pickles, BCOT Day Nursery, Basingstoke

5 Monitor team effectiveness, there is little point in putting in time and energy into team leadership and the team building process if the team is not achieving the goals effectively or if the team is unhappy with the process.

This can be broken down form a practical approach by looking at the stages of team development.

Stages of team development

Unlike child development, which is a forward trajectory, team development is a continual cycle. Obviously, you will want to be at stage four, (effective team performance), however at times you will move away for this stage for a variety of reasons. The effective leader knows at any time at what stage their team are at. They will also be able to identify on occasions when they are about to move from stage five (separation and closure) and put in place strategies to move the team back to stage four.

1. **Getting together as a team** this may happen through staff meetings, room meetings, briefings and importantly, also through social events. Getting together out of work is about getting to know the person, not just the work and the importance of shared experiences. This is particularly important when a new member of staff joins a team, they need to feel a sense of belonging and fully integrated. We can put the responsibility on them, but it is just as important for us to look at ways of supporting them to feel part of the team.

2. **Confronting conflict in the team** as long as conflict exists this is where you are stuck, you cannot move past this stage. Conflict is discussed separately in this Chapter on pages 23.

3. **Consensus and co-operation in the team** this is about agreeing working practices and deciding how the team will work. This links to Neugebauer's framework for team building, as described before.

4. **Effective team performance** this is the goal where you are aiming to be and where you hope to stay for significant chunks of time. In some multi team settings/schools, you may have individual teams at different stages. For the overall setting/school team to be at stage four, all the individual teams also need to be at stage four.

5. **Separation and closure** this concerns the events that might happen which move the team away from stage four. There can be a variety of reasons, some which can be anticipated and prepared for and others which are unexpected. The reason for the separation and closure will determine which stage you need to go back to and which stages you need to work through to return to stage four. Some of the causes may be:

- New member of staff (stages one and three)
- Maternity leave (can be planned for)
- Long term sick leave (unexpected)
- Compassionate leave (often unexpected)
- Conflict (stages two and three)
- New children (stage three)
- New policies and procedures (stage three)
- New manager (stages one and three).

Getting together as a team needs time and finding that time can be hard, but it is essential and it is about what you do when you get together. There will obviously be a need to focus on practice, development, policies and procedures, it is important though to have some fun and engage in some team building activities.

Stages of team development – where would I say my team are currently?

	My team is at this stage	How I know	What I need to do to move to stage four/maintain the team at stage four
STAGE ONE Getting together as a team			
STAGE TWO Confronting conflict in the team			
STAGE THREE Consensus and cooperation in the team.			
STAGE FOUR Effective team performance			
STAGE FIVE Separation and closure			

Team building fun

Here are some ideas for team building in staff meetings.

What I like about you
Everyone is given a blank piece of paper and on the bottom they write their name. They then pass the paper to the person on their right, who then writes something they like, a positive attribute, about that person. They fold over the paper to hide what they have written and pass on to the person on their right. By the end, everyone will end up with a piece of paper full of lovely comments about them.

Clear communication
Put everyone in pairs and ask them to sit back to back. Give one of the pair a lego model and the other a pile of bricks. The one with the model then has to describe to the one with the pile of bricks how to build the model. This is a great exercise for communication skills.

Can you create...
Ask each team to arrange themselves into the shape of a letter or number and then progress to forming a boat or a car. The only catch is they cannot talk, it has to be created non-verbally using body language to communicate to each other. This is great for seeing who takes the lead and who waits to be directed.

Egg carriage
Give each team 4 pages of newspaper, 1 carrier bag, 4 x30cm lengths of string and a small roll of sellotape. They have to try and create something that will transport an egg from the top of a window down to the floor, without the egg smashing. This is great for team work and negotiating and looking at different ideas and different ways in which people think.

Conflict

From time to time in every team there is conflict, and the conflict needs to be tackled head-on so it is properly eliminated.

Conflict is a disagreement or clash of ideas, principles or personalities. It breeds animosity and is often symptomatic of a breakdown in communication. We all tend to shy away from conflict, wanting to think it doesn't happen, but it can be extremely destructive and counterproductive. To approach conflict positively and manage it effectively, you need an understanding of how and why the particular conflict you face arose. It is usually either about an individual behaving in a way that causes resentment in others, or an issue between individuals.

Conflict is often caused by little things that escalate and cause difficulties and problems. Being aware of potential sources of conflict can help you either to prevent conflict from happening in the first place or nip it in the bud.

Once a conflict has been identified, what do you do? It's so easy to get things wrong, so first of all, let's consider what not to do.

Denial and withdrawal

When an issue is ignored in the hope that it will go away - it won't! The most likely outcome is that the problem will emerge later in a different form as a larger problem and therefore be harder to deal with.

Suppression and smoothing over

This is when a problem is acknowledged, but not fully addressed. For example, a practitioner is continually late. Rather than addressing this as unacceptable, you say, 'I know sometimes it can be difficult with the traffic, but you do really need to be here by 8.00am, if you can.' As a result, the practitioner makes no real effort to be on time and resentment increases amongst staff.

The aim of suppression or smoothing over is to move away from the problem as quickly as possible. This can be particularly damaging if there is an issue between team members, as the different perspectives and views are not explored, but merely hinted at. If the main issue is that there are two members of staff who are not getting on, it is as if the manager has said, 'Well, I know you're not getting on, but you have to, so off you go and play nicely!' The crux of the issue has not been addressed, no-one has had an opportunity to express their feelings and the problem will simply continue.

Power and dominance

When there is conflict, those involved need to be able to express how they feel, to feel they have been listened to and are no longer aggrieved. Using power and dominance shows a lack of respect for those concerned and for what they perceive to be a valid issue. It may force the individuals to agree or give way, but whatever caused the problem in the first place is still there.

Constructive approaches to conflict.

Having explored ineffective responses to conflict, we can now explore the process of how to respond effectively.

Assertion

This approach is particularly effective where there is potential for conflict to arise from the behaviour of an individual, such as lateness. Using an assertive approach will usually nip the problem in the bud before it has had time to become an issue for other members of the team. You need to plan what to say using the assertive format below:

When (description of the action, issue etc)...
Because (explanation of importance or relevance)...
I'd prefer (indication of alternative)...

'Over the past week you have been late four times. When you are late, this causes a problem in your room regarding ratios. Please ensure that you arrive by 8.00am.' Clear and to the point, with no room for misunderstanding.

Negotiation

Negotiation should be used when there is conflict between individuals that needs to be addressed. Firstly, you need to obtain a full explanation of the situation from all involved, so that there is a clear understanding of all viewpoints and feelings, if possible do this together so everything is out in the open. Together, you discuss a way forward that is realistic, practical and acceptable to all involved. It is essential that before the discussion begins, everyone has had the chance to say exactly how they feel; if not, even the tiniest issue that is held on to will emerge again at a later date.

Problem-solving

This approach is for the really tricky situations when a more direct approach is required. When using this approach, there are several steps that can be followed to clarify the real problem. Ask what is the real issue? And where does each party stand on the issue? If necessary, gather any facts and information, and together develop a number of alternative solutions through discussion, encouraging contributions from all.

If we always endeavor to tackle conflict directly however tricky, we will in the long term reap the benefits of having a happy and effective team. Dealing with it as quickly as possible also has a positive impact on team morale.

The strength of the team is integral to the strength of the setting/unit. The team needs to be valued and nurtured and the individuals need to feel like a team and see themselves as part of the jigsaw puzzle that makes the whole. There are a variety of ways to show your team that you value them:

- Effective supervision and appraisal
- Being open to ideas and suggestions
- Being proactive
- Have a team member of the months and reward with cinema tickets or vouchers. You could ask staff to vote for each other against a particular criteria e.g. doing nappies without complaining. Staff voting helps them to value each other
- Free chocolate Friday
- Listening to them and giving your time.

So, in summary an effective team achieves:

- An organised and effective setting, with structured deployment of staff
- Tasks are completed
- Consistency and continuity for the children
- Children's needs are met more effectively
- Raised standards
- Happy working environment
- Highly motivated staff/laughter
- Contented parents
- A positive atmosphere
- A drive, desire and commitment to continuous improvement
- Clear communication.

Motivation

When staff are motivated, they feel positive about their work. Here are examples of how staff can be motivated positively.

Influences creating positive feelings

Achievement: people like to achieve, and therefore want and favour anything that will help them to do so.

	Problem	Solution
Group structure/physical environment	Lack of communication within the setting between all practitioners and teams within rooms. Individuals may feel that they are not kept informed or receive information second hand.	Regular staff meetings and briefings, staff communication books, setting diary, approachability.
	Allegiances and subgroups form and then fall out, or rivalry develops.	A consistent pro-active and fair approach, careful forming of teams.
	Close teams and cliques may exclude others, for example, a team in one room being extremely close, causing others to feel left out.	Building links between teams, sharing and celebrating good practice.
	A general lack of understanding of job roles and the reasons behind the expectation of working in certain ways can lead to misunderstandings and discontent.	Ensure all practitioners have a clear understanding of their role and responsibilities within the setting and those of others, so they know where they fit in within the team as a whole.
	Lack of team time during the working day or at other times.	Try to provide time for teams to discuss, even if only briefly.
Time	Lack of planned time to complete assigned tasks, e.g. observations and planning.	Be supportive of this process and listen to concerns. Work through strategies for effective time management.
	Staff meetings without enough time for issues to be discussed fully.	Set a clear agenda prior to the meeting and stick to the order and if necessary allocate time for each issue.
	Timing of meetings.	Different days of the week will be easier than others for individuals to attend out of hours meetings, so don't always organise them for the same day.
	Poor time-keeping, e.g. individuals who are continually late in the morning or always late back from breaks.	Be seen to take action against any form of lateness.
	Long hours and shift work.	Acknowledge the difficulties and be as flexible as you can if someone needs to swap a shift.
	Use of unpaid time for work, such evenings and weekends.	If you ask staff to give up their own time, try to give something in return.
Parents	Difficult parents e.g. parents who question continually the practice and policy or collect their children late or try to bring their children in when ill.	Ensure that you give guidance and support to practitioners and if necessary step in to deal with the parents.
	Conflict with parents over issues within the setting.	Ensure that you give guidance and support to practitioners and if necessary step in to deal with the parents.
	Parental prejudices against individuals or ideas.	Be firm and assertive and explain practices and policies.
Goals and policies	Lack of understanding and awareness of policies and procedures.	Ensure practitioners understand and are aware of all policies, beginning with induction and continued awareness raising. Try to involve all staff in policy reviews.
	No common agreement regarding policies.	Involve staff teams in policy reviews.
	Individuals not following correct policies and procedures.	Be pro-active, take action and find out why they aren't following the policies and procedures.
The people	Personality clashes.	These do occur, consider if staff can move rooms or if it would be preferable to address the issue head on.
	Lack of respect for the leader/manager within the setting.	Discuss with the individual/s concerned and deal with any issues raised as a consequence.
	Inexperience vs experience.	Be a positive role model showing you value everyone's contribution.
	Age.	Sometimes younger members of staff are not respected by more mature staff and vice versa. Again be a positive role model showing everyone has a valuable contribution to make to the setting.
Change	Resistance to change (will eventually accept the change).	Think carefully about how you introduce any change. Remember the question people always ask first is how will this affect me? Answer that question before they have had time to ask it.
	Not accepting change.	Discuss clearly their contractual obligations if necessary and find out why they are not accepting the change.

Recognition: people like to know that they have achieved something and ideally they like to receive feedback that tells them so.

The work itself: everyone wants to enjoy their work and get a sense of satisfaction.

Responsibility: most people want this and getting it is usually seen as recognition of achievement.

Advancement: this is doing more, different and maybe more interesting things.

Growth: this is the opportunity to expand and develop skills.

Influences creating negative feelings

Supervision: if it is overbearing.

Working conditions: this can involve anything to do with the job.

Relationship with peers: any clashes, conflict or problem which will affect motivation.

Personal life: problems at home that can manifest themselves at work.

Status: unclear understanding of role and responsibility.

Motivating your staff – reflective practice

It is important to reflect on our motivational skills, by asking ourselves these questions. Can you answer them, ensuring each member of staff is included in at least one answer relating to the past week?

- **Achievement**
  What opportunities have I provided for staff to contribute new ideas and develop their capabilities?

- **Job interest**
  In what ways have I stressed the importance of the work of every member of staff?

- **Recognition**
  How often do I provide feedback about staff performance?

- **Status**
  How can I ensure the status and responsibility of staff is recognised and valued?

Developing your team - reflective practice questions

- How do you ensure that team members understand their roles and responsibilities?
- How do you support members of the team as they are working?
- How often do you carry out supervisions?
- How do you ensure that their work is interesting and valuable?
- Do you encourage team members to take on responsibility?
- How do you ensure that team members are able to extend their knowledge and experience?
- How do you ensure that team members feel that they are contributing to the effectiveness of the setting?
- How effective do you feel the system of appraisals is in your setting?

The Forming Storming Norming Performing team-development model

Dr Bruce Tuckman published his Forming Storming Norming Performing model in 1965. He added a fifth stage, Adjourning, in the 1970s.

Tuckman's model explains that as the team develops maturity and ability, relationships establish, and the leader changes leadership style. Beginning with a directing style, moving through coaching, then participating, finishing delegating and almost becoming detached.

At this point the team may produce a successor leader and the previous leader can move on to develop a new team.

The model progression can be linked to the stages of team development, as outlined on page 20 and 22, and with Neugebauer's framework for team building on page 21.

Staff meeting discussion points

- What does being part of a team mean?
- What makes an effective team?
- What are the positive things about being part of a team and is there anything negative?
- How can we make our team stronger?

Forming Storming Norming Performing team development model

The progression is:

1. **forming**
2. **storming**
3. **norming**
4. **performing**

Here are the features of each phase:

Stage 1 - forming (links with stages two and three of team development, leadership style: autocratic)
High dependence on leader for guidance and direction. Little agreement on team aims other than received from leader. Individual roles and responsibilities are unclear. Leader must be prepared to answer lots of questions about the team's purpose, objectives and external relationships. Processes are often ignored. Members test tolerance of system and leader. Leader directs.

Stage 2 - storming (links with stages two and three of team development, leadership style: autocratic)
Decisions don't come easily within group. Team members vie for position as they attempt to establish themselves in relation to other team members and the leader, who might receive challenges from team members. Clarity of purpose increases but plenty of uncertainties persist. Cliques and factions form and there may be power struggles. The team needs to be focused on its goals to avoid becoming distracted by relationships and emotional issues. Compromises may be required to enable progress.

Stage 3 - norming (links with stage 3 of team development, leadership style: democratic)
Agreement and consensus is largely formed among team, who respond well to facilitation by leader. Roles and responsibilities are clear and accepted. Big decisions are made by group agreement. Smaller decisions may be delegated to individuals or small teams within group. Commitment and unity is strong. The team may engage in fun and social activities. The team discusses and develops its processes and working style. There is general respect for the leader and some of leadership is more shared by the team. Leader facilitates and enables.

Stage 4 - performing (links with stage four of team development, leadership style: democratic/laissez faire)
The team is more strategically aware; the team knows clearly why it is doing what it is doing. The team has a shared vision and is able to stand on its own feet with no interference or participation from the leader. There is a focus on over-achieving goals, and the team makes most of the decisions against criteria agreed with the leader. The team has a high degree of autonomy. Disagreements occur but now they are resolved positively and necessary changes to processes and structure are made by the team. The team is able to work towards achieving the goal, and also to attend to relationship, style and process issues along the way. Team members look after each other. The team requires delegated tasks and projects from the leader. The team does not need to be instructed or assisted. Team members might ask for assistance from the leader with personal and interpersonal development.

Case study Leadership and development of the team

Charline Baker describes how she sees the role of the leader in relation to leading the team and developing staff.

I see it as leading by example, when in the rooms, modelling how to deal with situations e.g. challenging behaviour and talking through afterwards. Leading an activity, modelling interactions and extension of learning.

I need to know the strengths and areas for development for each member of staff. Regular observations support me with this understanding. I give staff feedback from observations, feeding into supervisions and set targets with time limits.

I reviewing their learning journals, giving feedback, so they can see what is working well and if there are any gaps or improvements to be made.

Good communication strategies are essential, including listening to them and being approachable.

I have a clear idea of where I want the nursery to go and I need to know that the team are on board, I do this by asking them how can we develop and improve, what are their ideas and suggestions? I listen and take on board their ideas and viewpoints.

Charline Baker, Play Days, Queens Road, Wimbledon.

What strategies do you have in place to prevent conflict?

Strategy for preventing conflict	How this works to help prevent conflict	What we do now	Steps to take to improve
■ Do you have effective communication strategies within the setting, to ensure all staff are kept informed and up to date, particularly part timers? Think about regular staff meetings and briefings, notice boards, staff newsletters, staff communication books, setting diary, robust systems of supervision and appraisal.	Staff will feel informed, valued and appreciated. They are then unlikely to feel disgruntled and excluded. Resentment can build if people feel left out or that they haven't been taken notice of or listened to. Supervisions and appraisal can be an opportunity for staff to express views and feelings, so niggles don't build or go unexpressed.		
■ How do you ensure all practitioners have a clear understanding of their job role and working practices? Can you be certain and confident in this knowledge and understanding?	Clear understanding of the role ensures they feel confident and sure of what they should be doing. When staff are unsure, tasks can go uncompleted and then resentment and conflict can build.		
■ How do you ensure that there are regular opportunities for staff to get together as a team?	This brings about cohesion and a sense of team and an opportunity to discuss issues and concerns.		
■ Do you advertise in advance the dates of your staff meetings? Do you ensure that they are not always on the same day, distribute the agenda in advance, keep to time and follow the agenda in the meeting and ensure that the minutes are available within 24 hours of the meeting?	Everyone needs to feel involved and included. By advertising staff meeting dates, staff can plan around the dates and ensure they are available. It avoids them being disgruntled if they do not have much notice. If they are always on the same day, a member of staff who find that day difficult may become resentful.		
■ Are you proactive? Do you deal quickly and effectively with any staffing issues, e.g. lateness.	If staff see you as being proactive they will respect you and resentment won't build about the member of staff who is never challenged for being later, so they are seen to 'get away with it'. If they can. 'Why shouldn't I?'		

Strategy for preventing conflict	How this works to help prevent conflict	What we do now	Steps to take to improve
■ How effective are you at supporting staff with difficult parents? What strategies do you use to offer support?	Parents can raise tricky issues sometimes and staff need to feel supported and not left to deal with alone to deal with these matters, as this can have a negative effect on morale.		
■ Do you involve all staff in policy reviews? How do you support staff to follow and understand all policies?	Helping to make everything easier for staff, also works to prevent conflict and I didn't know situations. Use questioning in rooms and discuss in staff meetings.		
■ Do you regularly undertake activities to encourage team building and team work?	Building more cohesion and understanding, aids communication and works to eliminate conflict.		
■ When recruiting new staff do you consider carefully how they will fit in with and compliment your current staff team?	Personality clashes or staff who do not have the right experience can be a major source of conflict. Getting the right mix of personalities and skills is essential.		
■ How do you promote and encourage an atmosphere of respect and tolerance in the setting?	Respect towards each other is critical. It can be helpful to spend time with staff thinking about what being a professional means, to help stop any nastiness between members of staff.		

Performance management

In the outstanding criteria for leadership and management, Ofsted mention 'incisive evaluation o staff performance', but what exactly is this 'incisive evaluation'? In practice, it means that a manager/leader should be fully aware of and understand each individual's strengths and areas for development. Part of that process involves supporting each member of staff to be aware of their own strengths. The incisive evaluation is about how you identify those strengths and areas for development and then the actions taken as a consequence. Reflection and the ability to assess performance and practice are a key component.

The cycle you have in place for supervision and appraisal, supported by observation of staff is an essential part of this process. Often, in settings, this can be a little hit and miss, as it seems an onerous and time-consuming task. However, performance and practice is much stronger where this process is embedded, as good practice is strengthened and developed and staff feel valued and empowered, poorer practice is tackled and staff are supported to develop in a variety of ways.

Additionally, there is a strengthened relationship between staff and management and a greater awareness and knowledge of what is happening in the setting for the manager.

Hints and tips for successful supervisions and appraisals

The key is spreading the appraisals and supervisions out across the year. Don't do them all at the same time, annual appraisal should be completed on the anniversary of someone starting their employment. In day nurseries, in particular, this can help space them out.

- Have a diary or calendar specifically for performance management and log in everyone's appraisal and supervision months
- Each month, identify who is due an appraisal or supervision, so you have a clear target
- How many supervisions should be completed? This will vary depending on whether you are an all year

round setting or follow the academic year. If you work roughly on the basis that everyone has something every 3 months, that would be an appraisal plus three supervisions. Sometimes a member of staff may need more frequent supervisions, for example during induction, or if you are supporting poor performance

- Staff observations should be carried out regularly and feedback given, and these can also be used to inform the supervision and appraisal
- Supervisions and appraisals can by carried out by managers, deputies and senior leaders. However, you need to ensure that everyone has at least one with the manager/leader
- In a day nursery it isn't always appropriate to delegate to a room leader, as they don't always have enough experience on measuring performance, but they can contribute their thoughts to the process. It can also be easier and more beneficial for a member of staff to reflect with someone they do not work with directly, especially if they have an issue with or concern about their room
- One of the biggest challenges, can be ensuring that everyone fully embraces the process and contributes. Take time in a staff meeting to go through the process and explain the purpose and what the expectations are regarding their contribution.

The difference between supervision and appraisal

Supervision is the regular contact between supervisor and their supervisee. This will give an opportunity to check up on how this member of staff is feeling from a well-being point of view, to chat about their key children, check progress and prioritise individual tasks, to provide and seek guidance and support and identify areas of work that need improving.

Appraisal is where job and individual development objectives are set. These are reviewed through the supervision process and additional targets can be set.

The benefits of supervision and appraisal from the perspective of the setting and the practitioner

For the setting:

- To support the practitioner in understanding the organisational values, and how they contribute to these through their practice and work
- To make sure children receive the highest quality care and provision and that their needs are met. The opportunity to chat over the key children provides practitioners with an opportunity for valuable reflection
- To ensure implementation of policies and procedures. Revisions to existing policies and procedures can be highlighted, as well as any new ones
- To improve internal communication through this one to one discussions. You can also use these as an opportunity to gain feedback generally
- To share responsibility as it provides an opportunity for delegation
- To assist in staff retention. The investment of time and open discussion means that staff feel valued and appreciated
- To lower rates of grievances, sickness and complaints, as there is an outlet to speak, and staff feel supported within their role
- To ensure that the practitioner meets the settings objectives and standards, and an opportunity to ensure clear understanding of them

Case study Supervision and appraisal cycle

Kerry Nihill describes her supervision and appraisal cycle.

Every three months each member of staff has a supervision and an appraisal on the anniversary of them joining the nursery. The supervision and appraisal cycle begins at the end of their probation.

In the supervision we chat about how they are feeling themselves and how they everything is going for them and their key children. Targets are set focusing on different aspects of practice at the end of the meeting. For each target we identify how they can be supported to achieve. It might be a training need which has to be addressed. After training I discuss with staff how they feel it has gone and they cascade in staff meetings.

The target might be about practice in the room e.g. interactions with the children. I would monitor them through observations as part of my room monitoring system. At the beginning it might be a twice weekly observation giving feedback and discussing if anything can be further developed.

If I see an improvement this monitoring is reduced so the practice can become further embedded through their own motivation. Some targets staff can be left to develop by themselves and feedback to me.

At the end of the supervision meeting, we read through the notes and targets and both sign the form. They have a copy and I have a copy which I file. For appraisal, I give them a form to complete before the meeting and we can then discuss to see if we feel the same about the staff performance.

Kerry Nihill, Play Days Nursery, Barons Court.

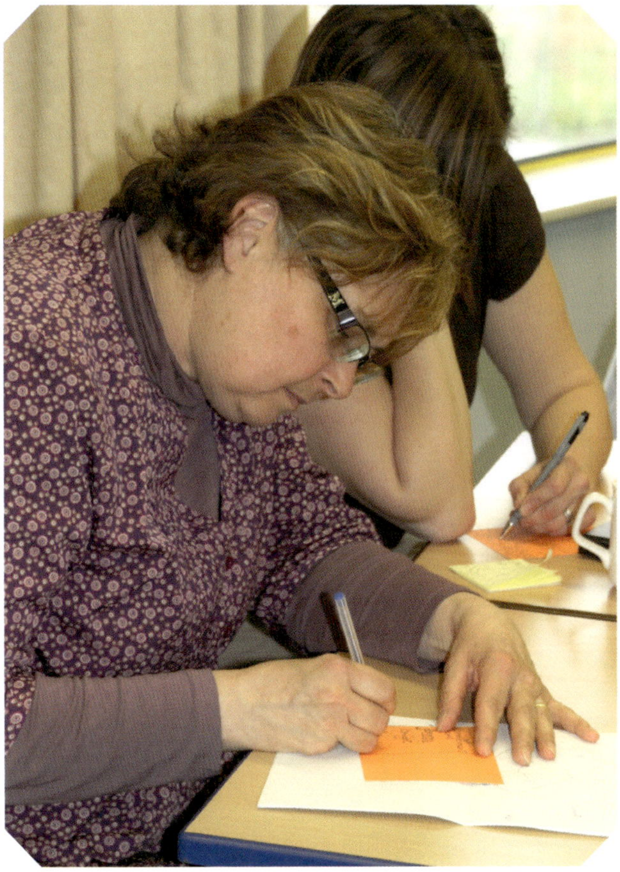

- To ensure that the practitioner has a manageable and appropriate workload. Does their job description reflect their job? Are there areas where they are struggling?

For the practitioner:

- To ensure that the practitioner is clear about their role, responsibilities and accountabilities
- To reflect on, analyse and evaluate their practice; some will need support with this through carefully worded open questions
- To set, agree and review targets
- To provide constructive feedback, clear understanding of strengths and, where practice needs to develop, how and why
- To ensure consistency of practice in the care of the children
- To value and appraise the practitioner's work
- To promote the health and well being of the practitioner, how are they generally
- To set clear boundaries for expected job performance

- To build self confidence, through being valued and praised
- To identify learning and training needs and consider how these can be met
- To improve team working
- To increase transparency and openness.

If completed regularly and appropriately the supervision and appraisal process will be supportive and result in motivated staff, who are driven to do and be the best as they are supported and enabled. Although time-consuming, the benefits are invaluable both for the individual and for the setting. Ultimately though there has to be trust and respect between everyone involved to ensure the process is as beneficial as possible.

Target setting

- Targets set need to be agreed and understood by all
- Practitioners should be able to talk about their targets after the appraisal/supervision
- They should be clear and specific, identifying what is to be achieved, how and by when
- They should be followed up in subsequent meetings and the impact identified, so the outcome can be tracked and any necessary additional support implemented.

What might be a target?

Targets will be specific to the individual and can be varied, here are some ideas and suggestions for targets:

- Training to develop an existing skill/strength or to support development of an area that needs improving
- A responsibility to develop a particular area of provision
- Could relate to completion of learning journals and quality of observations
- To develop parent partnership and involving them in children's learning
- To support another practitioner to develop their practice
- To research a theory
- To create an ideas bank.

Common barriers to quality supervision and appraisal

Supervision and appraisal can be an onerous task and it is easy to fall into pitfalls that prevent or affect effectiveness. It can be beneficial to reflect on the common barriers to effective supervisions and appraisals to ensure you are effective.

- Lack of organisation policies or standards on supervision and appraisal – a clear policy should be in place that is understood by all
- Lack of time and space – plan in advance and ensure you can go somewhere and not be disturbed
- Interruptions – part of the process is everyone respecting the right to an uninterrupted appraisal. Ensure the phone is answered by other staff and interruption happens only in emergency
- Poor recording of supervision – use well designed and easy to use and understand forms
- Inadequate training for supervisors – access training if available to help understand the process and how to ensure you everyone benefits. Training on supervision enables a clearer understanding of the process so it is more effective

- Lack of supervision for supervisors - ask for feedback on your supervisions. There is a proforma sheet included for use for practitioners to rate their supervision experience
- Unplanned, infrequent or lack of supervision - to be effective it needs to be regular and embedded. It is then a supportive and effective process and more welcomed and not something to be feared of.

Supervision and appraisal

Before the supervision session

1 Set supervision dates in advance so that they are planned and valued. Giving yourself and the practitioner time to reflect and complete any necessary paperwork. The paperwork acts as a prompt for reflection.

2 Plan for supervision, prioritise what needs to be discussed and encourage practitioners to do the same.

3 Review the supervision record of the previous session, and note items and action plans that need following up.

4 Check whether there are likely to be any unavoidable interruptions (these should really be exceptional).

5 Ensure the physical environment is laid out to allow the practitioner to express feelings, worries and be mindful of confidentiality issues. Think about light, fresh air, comfort and space.

During the session

1 Start the session on time. If you don't make supervision a priority, neither will the supervisee.

2 Confirm the agenda. Make sure the supervisee has had an opportunity to contribute to the agenda. During an appraisal, ensure you review the practitioner's job description.

3 Start the session by asking the supervisee how they are in order to promote their health and wellbeing and to put measures in place, if necessary, to offer support.

4 Use good communication techniques, for example open body language and good eye contact.

5 Listen and concentrate on what the person is saying without interruption. Ensure they have an opportunity to discuss any sensitive issues. Allow for pauses and silence to enable reflection and thought.

6 Use open questions - what, why, who, where, when and how, to explore ways of thinking creatively about a problem. Challenge where appropriate.

7 Be innovative in your approach, use scenarios to gauge thoughts, opinions and understanding.

8 Provide constructive feedback, praise achievements and encourage innovative ideas - giving more positive than critical comments.

9 Discuss and review work and practice issues. If there are any conflicts and problems relating to work, assist in providing a solution wherever possible.

10 Discuss and evaluate training and personal development needs.

11 Record the session by taking notes. You may wish to share responsibility for the recording, and give a copy of the record to the supervisee. Note any areas of disagreement, ensuring that both points of view are recorded.

After the session

1 Write up the notes and actions agreed, setting clear targets which are timebound.

2 Confirm accuracy with the practitioner.

3 Place a signed and dated copy of the notes in the supervisee's personal file, give them a copy to refer to as needed.

4 Agree dates for future sessions.

Staff observation

Observation of staff is a key component of the appraisal cycle. This needs to be completed by managers and leaders to enable a clear assessment of the key skills and abilities of the individual and an overview of the setting/unit as a whole. This means allocating time and being in the room not to be in ratio or interact or to model practice or to lead an activity, but to actually sit back and observe.

When observation is your key focus, you gain and see so much more than when you are moving between rooms. Often, managers say to me when I ask about observing staff, 'Oh I am always in and out of the rooms', that isn't the same though as actual observation time. I find in settings where observation of staff is strongly embedded, quality and consistency are much higher. Additionally, managers have a much stronger and broader perspective of setting and staff needs, strengths and areas for development.

There is no right or wrong way to observe staff, it is just important that it happens. You might observe a whole room or an individual. You might observe with a blank piece of paper, writing down what you see. It can be helpful to focus an observation on an activity and the practitioner leading the activity. Observation of particular times of the day, e.g. transition to lunch can be beneficial for highlighting how to ease that transition and develop practice. With regard to length of time to observe, it is really about what is needed and what is practical.

Rather than just a blank piece of paper you might also choose to have certain trigger questions for the observations or aspects of practice to focus on:

- Interactions with the children
- Extension of learning
- Variety of experiences available
- Supporting children's independence
- Key carer relationships
- Responses to children's interests and needs
- Management of behaviour
- Team work.

It is important to feedback as soon as possible to staff observed, to ease anxiety and to discuss any particular issues. If you wait or put off feeding back, it ceases to be of benefit and has little impact. General feedback about a room or the setting as a whole can also be done in meetings. It is important to be open about the process. It can, on occasion, be advisable to tell staff you will be observing in a room, but not necessarily that you will be focusing on one particular member of staff. That could make them nervous and affect their work. The process needs to work for everyone involved.

Benefits of staff observation

- An opportunity to reflect on the skills of individual practitioners
- Gives an overview of setting strengths and areas for development
- Supportive of professional development for practitioners
- Provides a forum for discussion about working practices
- An insight into issues and difficulties
- A proactive process for problem solving
- Feeds into the appraisal cycle
- Provides evidence to support development of practice

Case study Staff observation

Charline Baker describes how she uses observations of staff to develop practice.

During the observations I focus on interactions and activities as well as general practice. I look for the strengths and provide positive feedback and consider how I can help staff to further develop these strengths. I then look at where they need to improve and what I can offer them to improve. It might be internal or external training, it could be that another practitioner has a strength in that area and they can be assigned to mentor/coach the other member of staff. This means at the same time I developing a strength in one practitioner and whilst supporting an area for development in another practitioner.

If during observations I observe something that needs addressing right away, e.g. something they should know, not following a procedure, I would speak to them privately. This would be recorded on a cause for concern form if I have spoken to them about it before, if not it is just a verbal reminder. If I have to speak to a practitioner a third time, there would be an immediate consequence e.g. a verbal warning, if the severity of the breach warranted such action.

Charline Baker, Play Days, Queens Road, Wimbledon.

- Gives clear examples to use to provide positive feedback
- Shows staff they are valued and can be a motivator
- Can be an aid to identifying training needs.

Making a conscious effort to carry out observations, will have a positive impact on individuals and the provision as a whole. It is time well invested in the staff and the setting.

Meetings

Meetings, both whole staff and room meetings, provide a valuable opportunity for supporting performance management and professional development and should be seen as a key part of the process. They might be difficult to arrange, but are essential. Without regular meetings, there is no way of discussing and reviewing practice together, no opportunity for collaborative reflection or chance to discuss the children and review their progress. Meetings are fundamental for effective communication within the setting, without communication practice and organisational effectiveness can very quickly slip.

So, what are the benefits of meetings whether for the whole staff team or a team working within a room in a larger day nursery setting?

- A chance to share ideas
- Opportunity to review and evaluate practice and policies
- Everyone is involved if the meeting is managed properly
- Promotes teamwork and strengthens relationships
- Is an essential tool for effective communication
- An opportunity for open discussion and interaction to clarify ideas, procedures and practice
- An opportunity to deliver key messages, ensuring everyone knows and receives the same message
- It can be a forum to discuss and develop ethos and share common goals
- Staff can be publicly praised for good work and innovation
- Opportunity to cascade what has been learnt on training courses
- A chance to discuss together to solve a problem
- Issues that will benefit from open and honest discussion can be raised and it can give an opportunity for everyone to say what they think.

It is essential that a meeting agenda is published in advance, so staff know what will be discussed and minutes are distributed after. The minutes are important for recording agreements made regarding practice and for noting any targets that are set. These should be distributed, perhaps by email, with hard copies available. Each meeting should follow up on what was discussed at the previous meeting.

It is important to keep the meetings productive and focused. If the attitude to meetings in the setting is that they are a waste of time and nothing gets discussed or sorted they will become counterproductive. It may well be worth asking yourself or staff members how they see your meetings using reflective practice questions:

- Is there a clear purpose for meetings which is understood by all?
- How many staff attend meetings, is it always the same staff, how many don't attend, who and why?
- Is there sufficient preparation for the meeting?
- Is time used efficiently and effectively?
- Is there variety within meetings?
- Is the purpose of the meetings generally achieved?
- Is action to be taken, identified at meetings, followed up?

The answers and responses to these questions, can help to identify pitfalls and how to ensure meetings are successful. Your aim is to boost morale and for staff to come away from the meetings feeling motivated and positive about their work. What you don't want is for a meeting to bring cause for moans and grumbles.

The way to ensure that staff view meetings as positive is to run them in an organised and efficient style. First of all consider when and where meetings are held. In some settings it is best to run on the same day each month or in others it might work to run them on different days each month if that helps attendance.

Organisation of a meeting

Firstly, ensure you know the objective of the meeting and what you want it to achieve, and how that might happen.

An agenda for the meeting should be made available a few days in advance so that staff have an opportunity to think about issues they might like to raise or comments they wish to make about items on the agenda. It can also be useful to state on the agenda not only a definite start time, but also a finish time. A meeting of half an hour is much more palatable than one which looks like it is going to go on forever! Put in place a system whereby staff can add items to the agenda if they so wish, either under any other business or as a separate point. Many settings have a fixed meeting agenda, e.g.

- Attendance
- Safeguarding
- Children
- Planning and observations
- Health and Safety
- Policy, procedures and practice
- Professional development
- Training, both in-house or external
- A.O.B.

For each agenda this can be padded out clearly stating what is to be discussed, e.g. under policy, procedures and practice it might state a review of observation methods. Under professional development and training it may state who is going to feedback on the course they attended and the subject of the course. If you do have staff contributing to the meeting, make sure they have a specific time allocation, so they don't cause the meeting to overrun.

The chair of the meeting, usually the manager or leader in the setting, needs to ensure that the meeting starts on time. It can be beneficial to start the meeting by sharing good practice or a 'thank you'. Some settings have a thank you board in the staff room where they can stick a post it note, thanking a colleague for something they have done.

Once the meeting has begun, the chair needs to ensure that the agenda is followed and that the meeting keeps to time. This can be helped by clearly stating the aims, objectives and agenda at the beginning of the meeting. Someone needs to be responsible for taking the minutes, to be distributed afterwards.

The person leading the meeting needs to ensure that it is kept on track, so avoiding time wasting but also ensuring everyone who wants to speak has an opportunity to do so. Strategies may need to be used to encourage the quieter members of staff, those who are reluctant to speak. Preparation beforehand can help support this, as can inviting specific people to share their opinion or view.

Strategies may also need to be used in the case of dominant and vocal members of staff. Using names and thanking for contributions can help.

The goals of the meeting in terms of efficiency are:

- To ensure the discussion remains focused, constructive and keeping to the agenda of the meeting
- To ensure that the chair remains in charge and in control
- To ensure that there is only one discussion going on at a time
- To work to ensure that all points of view are given a respectful hearing, even if you and others don't agree with the viewpoint
- To keep the pace of the meeting flowing, remembering the time plan and agenda
- To keep the mood of the meeting positive and objective.

At the end of each agenda item, give a recap and summary of what has been discussed and agreed, ensuring everyone is clear and understands what they need to do, if applicable.

Close the meeting on time, agree the date and time of the next meeting and state when and where the minutes will be available for everyone, this should ideally be within 24 hours. If there is anything you need to do as a result of the meeting, ensure you do it within the specified time frame, or sooner, and ensure the minutes are available by the agreed date. The more positive the meeting experience is, the better the attendance and the likelihood of constructive contributions from all.

Training

Training is an essential part of performance management and can be accessed in a variety of formats. With budget issues and less accessible training, more online training is taking place, however it is important that everyone at some point as an opportunity to access training with other trainees and a trainer. This type of face to face training provides an opportunity for discussion and reflection which cannot be provided through an online portal.

Training can be completed in-house, delivered by a member of the team, or an outside trainer. Practitioners can attend training provided by the local authority and other organisations. Training can also be given on the job as a more senior member of staff works with and models good practice.

However the training is received, it is important that it is valued and that the individual knows why they are attending or undertaking it, that they have a clear idea of what they are hoping to learn or gain from the experience.

Training identified through the appraisal cycle will be meaningful and focused. Prior to doing the training, a focus form should be started so the individual can reflect on what they hope to achieve and then completed after the training, identifying what they gained and how this will impact on their practice. They should have an opportunity to share this in the setting.

There are many wide and varied benefits of training for practitioners:

- It can boost confidence
- Will develop skills and knowledge
- Can act as a motivator as practitioners return to their setting fired up with new ideas, which can permeate through the whole staff team
- Develops practice and therefore promotes best practice
- Helps to ensure knowledge is up to date
- Can provide an opportunity to share and discuss issues and practice with practitioners from other settings
- Provides an opportunity for reflective practice
- Is stimulating, thought-provoking and interesting
- If a practitioner is sent on a training course outside the setting, it shows that they are valued by the manager/leader, this needs to be consolidated though, by the practitioner being given opportunity to share what they have learnt.

Settings which invest in training and staff tend to be happier and more productive places to work, with better staff retention and a better provision for the children.

The benefits of training are also reflective of the general benefits of appraisal and supervision and therefore effective performance management. Through supervision and appraisal, you are demonstrating incisive evaluation of staff performance, as long as clear targets are set and staff are aware of those targets.

Qualities of an early years supervisor

- Empathetic
- Non-judgmental
- Good listener
- Anti-discriminatory
- Has good time keeping
- Reflective
- Respectful
- Honest
- Has integrity.

Rights of supervisees

- To receive effective and sensitive supervision
- To be treated in an anti-discriminatory manner
- To have their own feelings and opinions recognised
- To express their own opinion
- To learn from mistakes, to be unsure or to seek advice on what they don't know
- To be listen to
- To be briefed about changes.

Case study Using training to meet the needs of the team

The need for training was identified through room and staff observations and through individual staff supervisions. We found many staff were nervous when asked about how they 'teach' the children. Even those who do teach very well on a daily basis were failing to see what they do as 'teaching'. We felt that some learning opportunities were being missed during the course of everyday activities such as snack/lunch time, dressing/undressing and also that staff were missing opportunities to extend activities by following the children's lead and giving opportunities for problem solving and extended learning. There were missed opportunities too in terms of extending the children's language and comprehension by the introduction of new words and concepts. Sometimes the routines of the day were being allowed to dictate when and how the children learned.

During the course of the training there were lots of 'light-bulb moments' as some staff realised that they are actually effective teachers already. Others realised how easily they could extend children's learning quite simply, often just by listening to them and asking questions. Lots of opportunities were given to work in small groups and this was beneficial, especially as it gave less confident staff the opportunity to contribute and ask questions without feeling they were in the spotlight.

Following the training we re-visited some of the ideas during room meetings and incorporated some new concepts into planning. Sometimes, even if you have a strong staff team, which I believe we do, it's a good idea to provide the opportunity to refresh ideas and spend time as a team looking at what you do well and how you can continue to move forward.

Linda Newton, Kinders Mill Day Nursery, Hitchin.

Delegation

Delegation is often tricky and leaders can be reluctant to delegate to staff. Often, this is because you know that if *you* do it, it will be done on time and in a way you want it to be completed. Excuses for lack of delegation are often prevalent. However, delegation is a key component of staff development and if clear guidelines including a time frame are given, maybe the member of staff will complete a task in a different, but better way.

What is gained by delegation?

- It helps to ease your workload and therefore gives you time to concentrate on other important tasks
- Development of staff and full use of their skills
- Greater involvement and job satisfaction for staff
- Improved morale and mutual trust and confidence
- Decisions and actions made by those directly involved
- More effective organisation.

How to decide what to delegate.

Begin by asking yourself the following questions:

- What do I do now?
- Why should I do it?
- Should I keep it and why?
- To whom could I give the job/responsibility/task to?
- Who else should I be training to do it?

Begin by just identifying one simple task that can be delegated and build up from there.

Effective delegation:

- Establish reasonable goals
- Choose the right person and give them as much autonomy as possible
- Offer definite instructions to those to whom you are delegating
- Keep yourself accessible when required
- Share your thinking and goals, so they have background information
- Ensure they understand what is expected of them and how the results will be evaluated
- Let them know you will check progress
- Assign realistic dates for completion.

Staff meeting discussion points

- What is the purpose of supervision and appraisal?
- What do you think I am looking for in a staff observation?
- What does being a reflective practitioner mean?

Case study Training impact

Tracey Heayns discusses how she uses meetings to inform, support and develop her staff team.

We have whole staff meetings every 8 weeks, with room meetings in between and I have regular seniors meetings. For the staff meetings I put up an agenda in the staff room and they can add anything to it. The first half of the meeting is information and points that need to be raised from me.

The second half of the meeting is for professional development, recently we had a session on behaviour management or I had it over to the staff, as sometimes they need a forum to talk, to raise issues and to discuss what is going on in their room. This is about having a professional discussion which sometimes leads into training, as we share ideas about best practice.

Minutes are distributed after so it is clear what has been discussed and targets identified. Sometimes, it is the staff setting targets for me and it is my responsibility to get back to them. It might be looking into training or something in the setting. Targets might be for individuals, the nursery as whole or different rooms. This is record which can then be tracked to ensure targets are met.

I also send out a monthly staff memo either printed copies or via email. This highlights things that have come up. I detail what I am doing, particularly if I will be out of the setting, perhaps at another site. It might be about what the deputy is doing and if she needs any particular information. I update them about recruitment, anything else that is happening and what we will be looking at in our observations of the rooms and daily walk rounds.

I find that meetings have a positive impact as they boost morale, everyone is informed and kept in the loop, it is about the fact if you have the information you can do something about it. My team can see me taking action and being proactive and they are listened to and can see that something has changed or improved. There isn't always they result they wanted, but at least we have looked at it. Ultimately it is about improving practice and the quality of the provision.

Tracey Heayns, Busy Bees Montessori Nursery, Rushden.

Case study Supporting mental health and wellbeing

Supporting mental health in the workplace.

We ask our staff to complete well being questionnaires and we have more frequent well being meetings for staff who need it, so their voice could be heard and they were given time which really helped. We also have a folder of information on support groups.

We had two members of staff who were struggling, so we approached Bristol mental health for support. Claire came in and spoke with the two members of staff and myself, the manager, to see what we had in place and I that I was going on well being training.

Claire completed questionnaires with the two members of staff and from that, gave guidance on the right questions to ask to offer support. Claire came and visited every six weeks for six months, now as the staff are more settled she doesn't need to come in, she just phones for a catch up. During her visits Claire set us SMART goals for making reasonable adjustments to support the members of staff, with her support, we developed a 'staying well at work plan'.

Every two weeks the room leader and member of staff concerned have a well being meeting, providing performance feedback. They also complete a reflective log

I made sure we were doing the right thing investing in staff, it is about being a mindful employer and being prepared and informed.

Emma Base, Woodland House Day Nursery, Bristol

https://www.mind.org.uk/workplace/mental-health-at-work/taking-care-of-your-staff/useful-resources/

Your team members

This chart guides you through a reflection on each member of your team, reflecting on their skills and areas for development and how you can effectively support them.

Staff member	How are they supporting you in moving the setting forward?	Skills and strengths	Areas for development	How to further develop both

Training and development plan

Staff	Identified training and development need	How you plan to meet this need	Date to be achieved	Support required	Expected Impact (link to professional development records)	Actual Impact

Appraisal form - Part A

Please complete all answers and be as descriptive as possible. **PART A: To be completed by the employee** **NAME:** **DATE:**
What have you achieved in your role during the past year?
Does your job description accurately reflect your current duties? If not, please describe them here.
What do you consider to be your key skills and strengths?
In your opinion, what do you do best? Give examples.
Which parts of your job do you enjoy the most and why?
How effective do you feel you are in your key person role and ensuring that the needs of your key children are met?
What skills/area of work do you feel you need to improve upon the most and why?
Which parts of your job do you find the most difficult and why?
What are your personal goals for the next appraisal period?
Do you feel there is anything that could be done to help you meet these goals and perform more effectively?
Please comment on any areas/issues that have not been addressed.
Thank you for completing this form, please hand in your form to your appraiser one week before the arranged meeting date.

Appraisal form - Part B

PART B: To be completed by the appraiser prior to the meeting. **APPRAISEE:**	**DATE:** **APPRAISER:**
What has the appraisee achieved the past year/appraisal period?	
What are their key skills and strengths?	
How effective are they in their key person role and in meeting children's needs?	
Are there areas they can improve upon?	
What goals would you like to see achieved in this next period?	

Appraisal form - Part C

PART C: To be completed by the appraiser during the meeting			
What has been agreed as the key strengths and achievements over the last period?			
What has been agreed as the areas for improvement and development?			
How is this being supported?			
General comments and record of discussion.			
List any targets or training needs identified and how/when they are to be achieved.			
TARGET/TRAINING NEED	HOW IT WILL BE MET	BY WHEN	EVALUATION AND IMPACT ON PRACTICE
Date for next appraisal:			

Record of staff supervision meeting

EMPLOYEE NAME:	**DATE:**
SUPERVISOR:	**REVIEW DATE:**
ITEMS FOR DISCUSSION:	
Raised by supervisor (includes staff wellbeing):	
Raised by staff member:	
REVIEW OF PROGRESS ON ACTION FROM PREVIOUS SESSIONS:	
Action Points:	
KEY PERSON PRACTICE AND PERFORMANCE:	
(Observations, assessment, children's profiles, partnership with parents)	
Action Points:	
EFFECTIVE PRACTICE:	
Action Points:	
ANY SAFEGUARDING CONCERNS:	

ANY PROFESSIONAL DEVELOPMENT ISSUES:
Action Points:

ANY OTHER ISSUES:
Action Points:

TARGETS

TARGET	REASON	HOW TO ACHIEVE IT	BY WHEN	EVALUATION AND IMPACT ON PRACTICE

SIGNED EMPLOYEE:

SIGNED SUPERVISOR:

DATE:

Employee evaluation of supervision

Please evaluate your supervision using the rating scale below. If you scored 1 or 2 for any statement, please explain why in the box at the bottom.

1 strongly disagree
2 disagree
3 agree
4 strongly agree

STATEMENT	SCORE
My supervisor provides me with appropriate training opportunities.	
My supervisor clearly defines what they expect of me.	
My supervisor and I discuss how I can develop in my role and career.	
My supervisor listens well.	
My supervisor is available if I have a problem.	
My supervisor is a good problem solver.	
My supervisor gives clear and helpful feedback about how I am doing my job.	
My supervisor expresses appreciation of my work.	
My supervisor communicates clearly about plans for the setting.	
I understand how I fit into the team at work.	
My supervisor expresses appreciation for ideas and contributions.	

ADDITIONAL COMMENTS:

Performance management/Supervision jigsaw

The below illustrates how different components come together to give a complete and robust approach to performance management. Effective and supportive performance management is about more than just supervisions, that is just one part. It is all the parts together, which ensure practitioners are fully supported and as a consequence a setting is driving towards continual improvement and better outcomes for children.

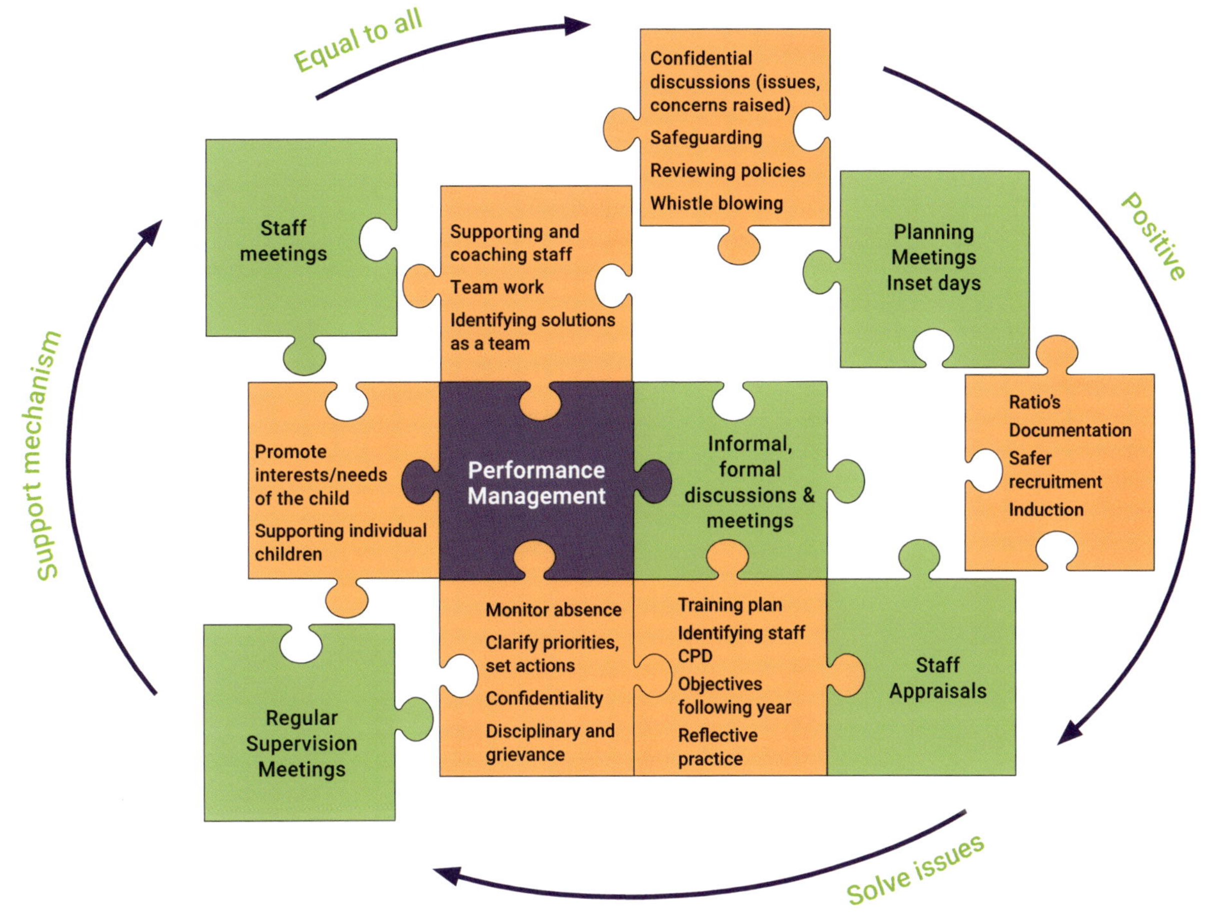

Source: www.somerset.gov.uk

Case study Staff swaps with other settings

I have recently set up a small discussion group with two other nursery school head teachers. During one of our meetings we discussed the importance of keeping our teachers inspired and discussed ways of evaluating our practice.

We decided that a possible way might be to carry out a staff swap between our settings. The idea is based upon a fully integrated approach whereby we literally swap one member of staff for another, usually for a morning, both equally qualified. When a staff member returns from a staff swap they complete a "Staff swap feedback form". This asks the practitioner to share details of what they have learnt, one thing they thought the other setting did well and then to suggest something that they will implement at our setting as a result. One example was introducing achievement certificates, they also brought in many ideas on outdoor play, using writing implements outside by taking clipboards to the garden; using tape measures outside to stimulate numerical language. I think it also empowers the practitioners and it improves their confidence to implement and introduce new ideas. The practitioners say they find it especially interesting seeing what resources other settings use and how they use them.

Lucinda Byron Evans, Young England Kindergarten, London

Monitoring children's progress and developing learning

Monitoring the experiences the children receive and the provision in general are a necessary and key part of the manager's role. This monitoring looks at a variety of aspects of the provision:

- Observations and assessments
- Quality of the activities and experiences provided, both inside and outside
- The organisation of the learning environment, both inside and outside
- The resources.

Observation of staff and room observations provide essential information for monitoring, but is not enough to fully answer the key questions. Those questions being:

- Are the children receiving a broad and balanced experience across all the areas of learning and development?
- Do staff have high expectations of the children and are they supported and enabled to reach their potential?
- Is learning extended and do children make progress?

How can this monitoring be carried out effectively? As previously mentioned, staff and room observations support the process, but there are other strategies, including:

- Reviewing and monitoring learning journeys, observations and assessments
- Daily walk rounds looking at deployment, ratios, health and safety and organisation of the environment

- Cohort analysis and evaluation
- Room audits/snapshots
- Choosing a child and tracking their experience over a session. You could follow more than one child at a time. What do they access, how are the supported by the practitioners, what is the quality of their learning experience?
- Spot checking the activities and experiences and identifying how the areas of learning and development are represented, and is there a balance?
- Reviewing planning and looking at how staff are responding to children and meeting their needs and reflecting their interests
- Carrying out a resource audit, what is used and what isn't used, how do staff use resources innovatively?
- Completing joint observations with practitioners on the room
- Completing time sample observations on a specific area/resource in the environment, to see how the children access it

- Keeping a monitoring/challenge book to make a note of and track common issues with provision and practice, by keeping a record of what you have raised it as an issue and with whom.

However you monitor the provision, it needs to be thorough and regular and shared with practitioners. The monitoring needs to be evaluated to draw conclusions so that targets for improvement can be set. This needs to involve the staff team or individual practitioners, as otherwise the monitoring will be ineffective in respect of improving practice. Discussion and asking for opinions on what you have observed or identified through monitoring is a key part of involving the staff team and if monitoring flags up issues with individuals then they need to be supported separately.

As a manager/leader you need to be certain that the children are having a high quality learning experience, which enables them to make progress. The cohort analysis and evaluation helps to highlight areas of progress and areas where progress is not as expected. From there you can work to identify if that is about the provision or about the observations being recorded.

Monitoring is a continual process and the broader the variety of methods used, the clearer the perspective you will get. Once it becomes fully embedded, the staff will see it as part of the general pattern of what happens and will be more open to it as well as involved.

They may have suggestions on how to develop the process and also ideas for improvement.

Staff meeting discussion points

- Take each area of learning and development, overall, what are the strengths and what need to develop in provision?
- What is a quality observation?
- Get staff to look at their room/the provision when the children aren't there, by kneeling down so they can see what the children see. What does this tell them about the learning environment?
- Take each Ofsed judgment, what do they think are the settings strengths, what do they think are the areas for development.

Case study Monitoring practice

Day Nursery Manager Lucy Meeson describes how she monitors practice in the different rooms of her large day nursery.

Each week, I focus on a different room, so each room gets monitored every six weeks. Over the week I go in at different times of the day and observe so I can see all aspects of the routine. I am looking at adult and child interactions, the environment, activities, the routine and check paper work e.g. medicine forms, accident and incident tracking.

At the end of the week I have a meeting with the whole room and discuss the main points of the observations giving feedback. Main points raised by the room leader and the practitioners are discussed so everyone is having a say.

At the end I give them a ticklist of actions needed to be done before the next monitoring. I find this works well as they have ownership of achieving the set once actions are completed. They have a copy of the list and I do as well, we all sign and date the list at the end of the feedback meeting.

When it comes to the next room monitoring, I ask for the list to see what they think they have completed and I see if I agree. We both keep copies of all the lists, as it shows the whole process and we can see the development and improvement.

As part of this process, each room has a self reflection file. Every month, each member of staff selects one activity they have completed with the children and reflect on how well it went. What worked, what could have been added, what could improve and if the children enjoyed it. These are then discussed as part of the room monitoring process.

Lucy Meeson, Play Days Nursery, Wimbledon Hill

Reflection on assessment and data collection

Monitoring children's assessment and progress is a key part of the leadership role, so it is important to reflect on the thoroughness and effectiveness of this monitoring.

These questions enable you to reflect on your approach.

Gathering information

- How do you ensure observations of day to day activity in a range of situations?
- How do you involve parents, children and other professionals?
- What information is important and shows the 'unique child'?
- How do you ensure recording systems are manageable?
- How do you support staff to reflect on observations to understand individual children?
- How is your understanding of the child's needs and development used to support progress?

Summarising information

- How do you record summaries?
- How do you summarise a child's learning and development?
- How do you quality assure summary assessments?
- How effective are your starting points assessments? How are parents involved?
- Which children will you track and why?
- How do you show progress?
- How do you ensure summaries show a holistic view of all areas of learning and development?
- How do you share progress summaries with parents?

Using information

- How do you organise the information?
- How do you analyse progress for specific groups of children?
- How do you analyse progress in all areas of learning?
- What other information about the children might you need to consider in order to understand their progress and needs?
- How do you identify and act on gaps in your provision in relation to practice, resources, organisation and environment?
- How do you use the information to support transitions?

What analysis needs to made?

- Are children as a group making progress over time?
- Are there particular children who are falling behind the age/stage expectations in one or more areas?
- Are there children whose learning and development is beyond age/stage expectations?
- Are children generally making more progress in some areas of learning than others – are there gaps?
- Do practitioners have sufficient understanding and skills in supporting children's learning?
- Does the physical environment support learning?
- Do staff have appropriate expectations for children's learning?
- Are there factors in common for children who are making slower progress?
- Are staff aware of the needs and abilities of children?

- Is there sufficient stimulation and challenge to support rapid progress for these children?
- Do staff have sufficient knowledge, and give attention to all areas of learning?
- Does the learning environment offer rich opportunities across all areas of learning?

What action might follow?

- Plan for team and individual CPD in improvement plan and performance management
- Develop indoor and outdoor provision with appropriate resources
- Identify and implement strategies to meet the children's needs
- Obtain support from partner professionals, ensure SEN support systems are robust and practitioners supported to meet individual needs
- Review and develop observational assessment and responsive planning
- Arrange CPD on identified areas of learning
- Review routines and planning.

From Progress Matters: Reviewing and Enhancing Young Children's Development (National Strategies 2009).

Provision checker

ROOM: PRACTITIONERS: CHECK COMPLETED BY:	DATE:

	Continuous Provisions		Planned activities	
	Inside	Outside	Inside	Outside
Personal, Social and Emotional Development				
Communication and Language				
Physical Development				
Literacy				
Mathematics				
Understanding the World				
Expressive Arts and Design				

EMPLOYEE NAME: TARGETS FOR ACTION:	TARGET: TO BE COMPLETED BY:

Room snapshot

	Evidence	Comments
Is there a range and variety of activities available that are age/ stage appropriate?		
Are activities set out at different levels?		
Do activities encourage exploration and investigation?		
Are resources up to date and relevant?		
Can children initiate their own play through free choice?		
Are staff interacting with the children as appropriate?		
Was learning being extended?		
Are resources clearly labelled with words and pictures?		
Are all the staff interacting and engaging with the children?		
Were there examples of stimulation in place to encourage interest and curiosity?		
Are children supported to be independent and look after their own needs?		
Is the register completed?		
Do the children appear to be happy and engaged?		

	Evidence	Comments
Do children and adults appear to have a sense of pride in this setting?		
Are there displays of children's work - are these clearly labelled perhaps with the child's photo?		
Are nappy charts and sleep charts completed?		
Would all children feel that they belong here?		
Are staff easily identifiable?		
Is there a visual routine?		
Are there any children in damp clothing or with runny noses?		
Are the children's key person and second key person identified?		
Do children have free access to drinking water?		
Are the toilets well stocked with soap, handtowels and toilet paper etc?		
Is there access to natural materials?		
Are all cultures reflected?		
Is there free flow play indoors and outdoors?		

EMPLOYEE NAME:	**TARGET:**
TARGETS FOR ACTION:	**TO BE COMPLETED BY:**

Case study Supporting children with additional needs

Sarah Wynne Jones describes how children with additional needs are supported in her nursery.

Through our tracking, if we see a child is not developing at the expected pace, the key carer and other practitioners in the room will complete additional observations. They will then speak to one of our SENCOs who will observe the child. If they feel the child needs extra support, they will meet with the child's parents to discuss their concerns.

The purpose of the meeting is not only to discuss the concern, but to also suggest that the local authority Early Years SEN advisory teacher comes out to the setting to observe. Sometimes parents can be reluctant and resistant understandably, we stress they are not coming in to judge but there to support nursery staff to ensure they are doing everything possible to support the child. If parents refuse we keep up the discussion with them and continue to support as best we can. If the parents agrees a form is completed and a meeting arranged.

The nursery manager and SENCO have an initial meeting with the parents and the EY SEN advisory teacher to explain the process. After the meeting the advisory teacher will observe the child and write up a report. There is then another meeting where they give feedback about what we can do in the nursery and we draw up an individual support plan, this will usually have 3 or less targets. The nursery SENCO will then work with the key carer to plan activities and how to offer one to one support.

Sometimes the local authority Early Years Specialist practitioner comes in with props and resources to support us to have the right tools and to model good practice. We have also had speech therapists coming in to work with children in their rooms and to give advice and tips.

On occasions with some children we have used a specialised tracker to monitor progress which has smaller steps as we felt it was more appropriate.

When the children leave us to start school we complete a specialist transition form so the school has complete knowledge about the child and we invite the teacher into the setting to observe the child.

Every three months we organise a review meeting to see if the targets have been reached. If they haven't been reached, we look to see if they need to be modified in anyway. Once the targets have been reached we set new ones. Throughout the SENCO continues to support the key carer.

We have two SENCOs as we are a large setting and there is a lot of paperwork evidence to collate, with reports, observations and evidence tracking.

Sarah Wynne Jones, Play Days Nursery, Chiswick

Case study Reviewing learning journeys

After joining a nursery as a manager, I began to review the learning journeys already in place in the nursery. I found that the staff were using lengthy sheets with very brief observations that contained hardly any detail, focus or analysis. I decided we needed to change them and make them more of a diary with observations linking to photos, if appropriate, and to the stages of learning and development. This would enable the observations to be more focused and detailed and give a clearer all round view of the child.

I also introduced a termly record of development and transition forms, in roughly the same style as the 2 year old check already in use. This was to ensure that the staff would be confident to complete the new forms as they were in a familiar format.

I created a mock up of the new style learning journey, as some staff needed to visualise what it would look like to be confident in implementing it. I introduced the new format at a staff meeting, with opportunity for staff to ask questions, so the new format could be introduced immediately.

After just 2 -3 months the new style was embedded for all staff.

Rebecca Pickles, BCOT Day Nursery, Basingstoke.

Case study Monitoring learning journals

Day Nursery Manager Lucy Meeson describes how she monitors leaning journals.

Every 2-3 months I ask for all the children's learning journals. I have a chart I complete for each key person, as I go through their profiles adding each of their key children's names. I check to see if the 'all about me' form is fully completed with photos, the local authority tracking sheet is up to date and completed correctly, as well as 2 year old checks and summary assessments completed.

I then look at the observations to see how they are written, how they are evaluated and how they are linked to the planning. I have a notes page where I write down anything they need to work on e.g. 'as discussed previously, observations should be written as if you are watching the child'.

I then go through the sheet and feedback to each individual member staff and we discuss the points and then we both sign and date. They have a copy and I have a copy. At the next monitoring I go through the previous sheet to see what has been done. When I see improvement I know they have understood, are listening to me and taken notice of what we have discussed.

By looking at each key person's profiles together I can identify trends through all of their profiles. Through the tracking and record keeping I can see where they have improved or if they slip back as it can go in waves. If they need further training, I will write this at the top of the sheet. I may get to the point with some where there are no notes. If I felt a practitioner was struggling, I would look at their profiles more frequently, every 2- 3 weeks.

Lucy Meeson, Play Days Nursery, Wimbledon Hill

Case study Pupil Premium funding

Caroline Sewell describes how she spends her EYPP funding.

I keep all my records and evidence tracking in a folder and each term have a different focus. With our most recent funding I spent it on a light box to support both ICT and maths. Although we had equipment for both they weren't being used and I wanted to introduce a different focus. With the light box I bought numbers and shapes which light up, which the children have really enjoyed playing with. This developed into extended office area with telephones and keyboards that the children access daily and is never empty.

I can already see an improvement through the utilisation of the resources and the enthusiasm of the children. This is supported with observations and photos. I know that when I track those children I will see an improvement in their progress.

In the past we have used EYPP funding to provide healthy lunches for children and to enable some to access extra sports lessons in the nursery. This spending was about healthy lifestyle more than focused development, however both impacted on their learning.

We have a proportion of traveller children in the nursery and I have used their EYPP funding to develop outdoor provision. Traveller children find being inside restrictive, as they are so used to being outside. We specifically developed and introduced a mud kitchen area, to support learning outside as pretend play is something they enjoy. The children really enjoyed the activity and were engaged and we found they invited other children into their play and began to talk about their experiences at home. This supported them socially and with their language.

We used the mud kitchen and bikes to gradually support them in feeling comfortable in both the inside and outside environments, by utilising the canopy area that we have attached to the nursery building, as a stepping stone between the two environments.

Caroline Sewell, Redbourne House Day Nursery.

Working in partnership

Partnership working is a key part of the leadership role, be that with parents, outside agencies and professionals or community partners. The largest aspect of partnership working, is that with parents and carers, which can sometimes be challenging.

We live in a diverse society, with a wide variety of family and parent models. All with their own set of needs and we need to ensure that we are fully inclusive. Every family has its own culture, traditions, lifestyle and values. We may not understand the lifestyle or the values of the family, but we must always show respect. That has to be our starting point.

As settings, we need to recognise the important role that parents play in their child's life, and how positive relationships with them benefit the child, the setting and the parents themselves. The relationship we establish with the child and their family enhances all aspects of the child's experience in the setting. The positive relationships that surround the child, enable learning and development to take place.

Parents want practitioners who are confident and well-informed, but also able to get along with them and show an interest in them and their lives. When practitioners and parents work together with an ethos of partnership, with each contributing their particular expertise and knowledge, this helps in turn to overcome barriers that can prevent parents from seeking support.

It can be helpful to consider what barriers might exist to parental engagement:

Emotional barriers

These are barriers parents may have relating to involvement. These can be triggered by an emotional response and often related to self esteem. For example:

- Fear of being judged by other parents and practitioners.
- Comfort level (feel intimidated in groups/meetings, low self esteem, low confidence.

- Fear of feeling 'out of place'
- Feeling that they are 'not educated enough' and assuming that what they have to say doesn't really matter
- Feeling overwhelmed by parenthood and having little energy or 'mental space' to give to anything else
- Attitude or perceived attitude of individual members of staff (being undermined, not being valued).

To help overcome these barriers, you need to ensure you are being sensitive and actively listening to the parents, looking at ways to involve and include parents in a relaxed manner. It is about your manner and approach.

Interest barrier

- Not understanding the value, relevance or purpose (what's in it for me/my child?).

By explaining to parents and valuing their input from the start, this can help to overcome this barrier. Valuing parental input may negate the need to explain, as the importance becomes self evident.

Skills and language barrier

- Literacy barriers (filling in questionnaires and forms, reading information leaflets etc)
- Communication skills (speaking in groups or at meetings, negotiation, resolution etc)
- Learning difficulties or disabilities (dyslexia, vision impairment, hearing impairment etc)
- Language barriers (non-English speakers, speakers of English as an additional language).

Where these barriers might exist you need to ensure you have strategies in place to help, considering individual needs and, often, confidence. Reflecting on what it is like to be a parent of a child in your setting can be aid to engaging parents, as you are enabling yourself to look with perspective.

For many settings, parental engagement begins with home visits which can provide a unique insight into the child's life and begin to establish the key foundations of the relationship with the parents, which can be built upon. It is once the child begins in the setting that we need to reflect on our practices looking at the ways in which we can reach all parents. Starting points assessments need to be completed and shared in conjunction with parents, so you can identify if there are any discrepancies between what the child enjoys and can do at the setting. Remember, you can always scribe for the parent and if they have nothing to say, ensure they sign the assessment, if paper-based.

In the past few years many settings and schools have moved to using a tablet-based system for recording children's observations and for sharing information with parents. Having made this switch, many settings have reported vastly improved parental engagement. Parents are able to view and comment on their child's observations and can add their own observations and in some instances videos of their child. This process actively engages the parents in a practical way and values their input.

This is obviously not possible for all settings perhaps because of WiFi issues or parents who are unable to access the internet. Observations and assessments still need to be shared with parents, this is to enable on-going discussion about their child's progress and to encourage their contributions. Many settings operate a shared WOW moments system where parents can share what their child has done. Regularly share observations with parents, either through parents evenings or informal chats, and encourage them to do their own observations of their children. This could be simply sharing with you a photo they have taken and telling you verbally what their child did, which will help include parents for whom writing something down might be difficult. The interaction and sharing is the key.

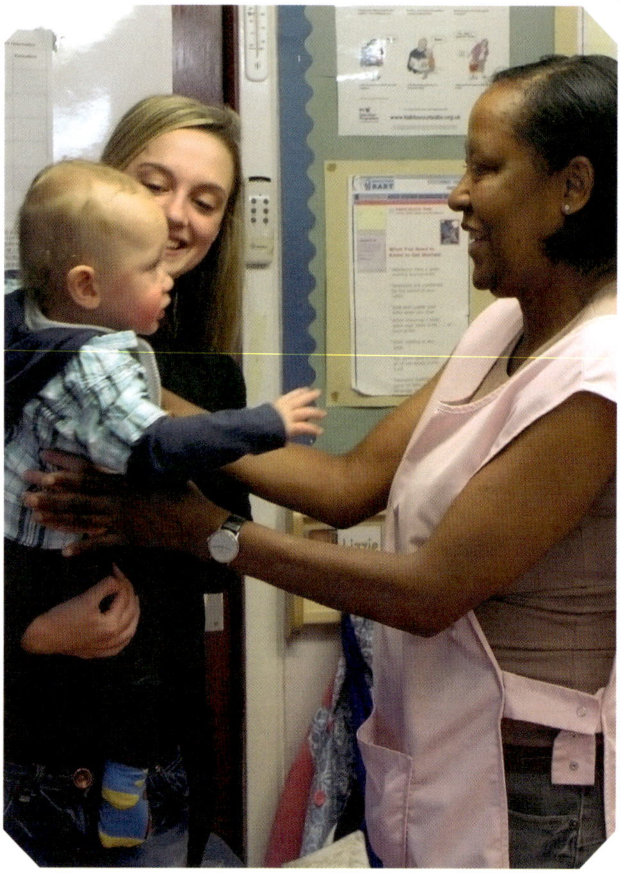

Case study Learning together scrapbooks

We have a learning together scrap book for each child and their family. Inside we explain the purpose as follows:

Every one of you does wonderful things with your child that helps them to learn and helps us to do our jobs at nursery. This book is to celebrate all those lovely experiences you share with your child. Every other Friday we will send this book home with your child to record they things you do when your child is not in nursery. You can record in a variety of ways – such as by gluing in tickets, receipts, photos, pictures and leaflets – how you display these things is up to you.

All we ask is that you send them back into nursery when you have added things to it, we will then read and return them to you.

Every so often I put in a task relating to what we have done in nursery, for example:

In nursery we have been learning about celebrations such as Diwali and Bonfire Night, as well as about Autumn. Please use these 2 pages to tell us what you have been celebrating at home recently.

The parents then choose how they record the work. We have had one family sharing their Diwali celebrations, another about St Nicholas Day, others cake recipes from various countries. We find out so much about what happens at home and it gives us so much to talk about with the children. They take a lot of pride in the scrapbooks and we display them alongside our learning journeys.

We stress to families it is not compulsory and they can dip in and out adding to them when they wish. We have about 2/3 of families that do them regularly and a few more that dip in and out. Some of the families that engage are ones I least expected to be involved. I have one family where they 2 year old is the oldest of three children and her parents are very young and they have engaged the most. We get so many differing stories and it is great for breaking down language barriers with EAL families.

Stephanie Metcalfe, Beechwood Primary School, Crewe

When sharing summative assessments/termly reports with parents, be sure to identify how the setting and home can work together to support the child, ensuring you provide clear examples and explaining where next for the child.

In addition there are other ways to involve and engage parents:

- Post updates about what has been happening via social media, either on Facebook or through a Twitter account
- Put suggestions on displays of supporting activities/discussions for parents to have at home with their children linking with the display
- Include ideas on newsletters as to how parents can support their child at home, emailing newsletters can be the most effective way of distributing
- Set up a library of activity card suggestions e.g. play dough recipes, activity idea measuring how tall someone is lying on the floor using socks etc
- Make some simple games which parents can take home
- Encourage parents to share photos of their children enjoying these activities at home, which can then be printed or loaded onto a digital photo frame and shared
- Invite parents or carers in to share skills, special recipes, family interests and to participate in reading stories to the children.

Multi agency working can sometimes be needed for some children, often for those with additional needs and for any with whom social services are involved. Open communication is the key in these instances, the sharing of knowledge, information, insights and observation of the children so they can be best supported.

Often professionals with specific skills may come into the setting to observe certain children and to offer support, advice and tips to practitioners working with particular children. These practitioners need to feel supported by their manager in these endeavours and feedback should always be invited by the manager after these visits or meetings to see how the practitioner is feeling.

It is also good practice to integrate the setting as part of the wider community. There are a variety of different ways in which this can be achieved. As a manager you can create links either through local children's centres, other settings or by attending cluster meetings.

This can be helpful for keeping up to date, sharing best practice and working together with other professionals to support the children and their families.

Being part of community events, is a great way to get your name out there and even better if the children can be involved in some way. Many settings are working with local retirement homes or drop in centres where the children are visiting to chat and perhaps paint pictures with the elderly or performing with them.

In some countries including the USA, Canada and Singapore, this has gone one step further and childcare and senior centres share the same building.

If you have local shops near you, making regular visits can build up a working relationships with the staff there and if they are small and independent can provide an interesting experience for the children. Local libraries are often keen to be involved with early years settings. Also visiting different places of worship within the local area can be valuable for broadening experiences and creating links. In the supporting case studies for this chapter, you will read about a visit to a football stadium and settings who go on the train weekly to participate in beach school.

Involving parents with play

Different parents will respond to different ideas and suggestions, here are examples of how you can support parents to be involved in their children's play.

- Take time to get to know parents so you can share information and ideas that are appropriate to their level of confidence, as well as relevant to their interests, culture and family life
- Treat parents as partners in their children's learning – parents are more likely to listen to information and advice if they feel respected and valued
- Be aware of parents' feelings and the pressures they may be under. Acknowledge their concerns rather than dismissing them
- Model positive interaction with children – for instance talk to the child about what they have been doing during

Case study Trip to football stadium

Taking children for local walks has always been part of the daily routine for our nursery and we have developed this to taking children on public transport further afield to give children new and exciting experiences.

The trip to Blackpool Football Stadium was arranged with the football coach from Blackpool Football Club who delivers weekly football lessons in the nursery. I had seen on social media a photo of a group of children on a stadium visit and thought it would be a fantastic opportunity for our children to explore an iconic part of the local community. The plan was to take the children on the bus, have a tour of the football stadium by the coach and then have their normal football lesson at the stadium, with a break for a snack, which we took with us.

The children were given a full tour of the stadium, including the stands, the executive boxes, the dugout, the trophy room and the pitch. They even got to sit and have their snack in the dugout. Once they had finished their tour and snack they then had a football lesson, which included doing a penalty shoot-out at the end.

The trip was very easy to organise, just a matter of arranging dates and checking bus timetables and writing a permission slip for parents.

We are lucky in our area that we have good public transport links as often coach travel is prohibitively expensive and has put us off planning trips in the past. I wanted all children to be able to take part in the trip and for no child to be excluded because of cost. In fact, I did not charge parents for the trip as I had only to pay for the bus fare for the adults.

The children were very excited about going on the trip and especially about going on the bus. Several parents said their child had not been on a bus before so those children were experiencing this for the first time, which they found very exciting. The children have now discussed going on a train, as we also live near to the railway station, and the train goes to the beach.

I feel that because we take our children out regularly they have good awareness of road safety, and of listening and following instructions. We often get comments from members of the public about how well behaved our children are. It is also good advertising as the children all wear high-vis vests bearing the nursery logo.

I was very pleased that all parents gave permission for their children to go on the trip and none expressed any concerns about the safety of their children. This confidence that the parents have in the staff's ability to keep their children safe has undoubtedly given all staff, especially the new members of the team, the confidence to continue to plan and deliver trips and outings as part of the nursery experience.

Michelle Wood, Childcare Manager, Happy Days Ansdell

Case study Working with a local children's centre

Every six months, Rachel from our local children's centre visits and sets us a target for developing practice. Rachel asks questions reflecting a specific focus to help identify our target. One recent focus was on 'disadvantaged children'. From the reflection questions and discussion, we discovered there were many ways to interpret disadvantage. With each reflective question you have to consider the evidence you have as you decide if the nursery is emerging, in place or embedded in each area. The questions asked were:

1. What is your setting's understanding of the term children at a disadvantage and how do you identify them?
2. What strategies do you have in place to address their needs?
3. How are you monitoring their progress?
4. If you have 2 year olds in your setting how do you use information collected?

We completed another reflection focused on communication and language. From that we introduced literacy walks, use of more visual aids and tools to support language and a focus on the importance of repetition with books.

We used videos to look at practice and from that, we identified that during singing, some staff were getting carried away and singing too fast for the children. We slowed down singing and discovered that the children were better able to join in and finish the words

Our environment improved as we introduced small things to improve literacy. We now have story boxes with real objects including windscreen wipers and a steering wheel, these come from interests of the children, in this instance with the song 'The Wheels on the Bus'. This has spiralled and staff are highly motivated to find the best and most unusual resources in charity shops, as a stimulus for language with the children.

Emma Base, Woodland House Day Nursery, Bristol

the day and praise them in front of their parent when they arrive to collect their child. Chatting to children, praising them and showing an interest in their play are all vital ways with which parents can support their learning and development. Modelling is a key practitioner skill that gives parents an opportunity to hear what positive communication sounds like – and motivates them to communicate in this way by seeing how their child responds to attention and praise

- Talk to parents about what activities their child has enjoyed doing during the day and share information about what they have been learning through this kind of play activity and how it could be followed up at home
- Talk to parents about what their child enjoys doing at home. Let them know how important they are for their child's learning and explore how they could join in play activities at home together
- Reassure parents that their attention and time matter more to children than expensive toys. Suggest play ideas that don't cost money – using household items, messy play with dough, singing simple rhymes etc.
- Help parents to see that the aim of playing with their child is to have fun together and build their child's confidence by allowing them to take the lead. Many parents use play as an opportunity to 'teach' their children a new skill and may need to be reassured that children learn best at their own pace
- Involve parents in activities to support home learning where appropriate
- Share information about stages of child development so that parents have realistic expectations of what their children can do
- Let parents know if their child talked about a play activity that they did at home, and how much they seemed to enjoy what they did with their parent.

Staff meeting discussion points

- What do they think are parents expectations of the setting? How can these expectations be managed, thinking about what is it like to be a parent of a child in your setting.
- How can we become more involved in the community?
- How effective are we at supporting children with additional needs? What evidence do we have of our effectiveness?

Room snapshot

Factors that support parent engagement	Fully implemented How do you know?	Could do more, explain
Are all staff aware of the importance of parental involvement in children's learning and development?		
Do parents feel welcomed and valued by all staff?		
Do staff work within an ethos of partnership with and respect for parents?		
Are there opportunities for staff to develop their relationship skills and confidence in engaging with parents?		
Is there a keycarer for each family and do parents know who their keycarer is?		
Do all staff take the time to chat to parents and get to know them and their family when they bring and collect their children?		
Do staff take the time to find out about personal issues that may affect parent-child relationship such as financial worries, relationship breakdown etc?		
Are staff aware of issues that could affect a parent's involvement in learning e.g. languages spoken at home, literacy etc?		
Are resources and information for parents displayed and available in the childcare setting?		

Case study Working with traveller families

Caroline Sewell of Redbourne House Day Nursery describes her experience working with traveller families. "We started having children from the travelling community attending the nursery when 2 year old funding was introduced. Initially we found it hard to build a relationship with the parents as they would drop and go. Soon after the children started Tracy from our local children's centre got in touch and we began to work together. With the traveller families you have to build up trust and work with them as they can be protective.

Tracy took me to their site and introduced me. I remember the children all flocked to Tracy. She introduced me to everyone and showed me where they live. This gave me a deeper understanding and insight. Tracy and I built up our working relationship and if any child didn't attend I would update her or there were behaviour issues, she would come into the nursery and carry out joint observations with me. We could then liaise and develop strategies.

Over time the families began to trust me and I began to get to know them and understand the patterns and cycles in their lives. Often the men would go away to work and on their return we would see a change in the children's behaviour and instances of domestic violence and pregnancy.

The benefits for the children of attending the nursery are immense. It helps to set the routine and pattern for school attendance and many of the boys stop attending school after year 6. It is supportive of their all round development, particularly in relation to language. This issue with language has a knock on effect with attention seeking behaviour, linked with frustration through speech and inability to express themselves.

With one particular child who needed specific support, Mum came in for a meeting and Tracy and I went on a special home visit. This enabled me to see what his home life was like and significant factors relating to sleep, such as sharing a double bed with his two brothers. We could then work more effectively to set boundaries and bring about stability for him in the nursery. If you understand the lifestyle it makes everything easier.

It has taken a long time to build up the trust and respect and whilst the families might not like some of our boundaries, they understand and conform. In a recent Ofsted inspection, one of the mothers spoke to the inspector which is a wonderful endorsement of how far we have come with our work with these families.

Case study Narrowing the gap

We track the children's progress through tracking sheets and complete assessments three times a year. We identify if children are emerging, developing or confident. We then look at a comparison with different groups SEN, summer born, EAL, boys, girls and attendance.

These are then moderated and we can then pick up if any groups are making more or less progress. We identified that EAL children were not showing as much progress in Communication and Language compared with other children in the nursery.

We decided then to make communication and language a focus across the nursery, as we felt in general there was a lack of emphasis. We appointed a communication and language lead in the nursery. We planned more focused activities, made the environment more literary rich with words from different languages spoken in the nursery and identified key words to use from parents to support children's understanding.

When we did the next racking, we discovered that the gap had narrowed and that the children had made rapid progress. We could see that our change in approach and focus had a positive impact.

We also identified that moving and handling and specifically mark making for a group of boys aged 18 months to 2 years was not where it should be, so we made physical development a focus, reflecting their interest in balls and cars. They became more interested and we gave focus to this prime area for the under 2's and it helped the transition into the next room. Again we could see at the next tracking that progress had been made.

To support this process, we held staff meetings on moderation and tracking, so staff had an opportunity to discuss what they were observing and discovering about the children. This also enabled us to track the impact on the children.

Lauren Matthews, Woodland House Day Nursery, Bristol.

Safeguarding

The safeguarding and prevent responsibilities the leader has in a setting are broad, and it is essential that there is clear understanding of all it involves and that the understanding and awareness is shared with all staff as necessary. Ultimately though, the responsibility lies with the manager. It is about creating a culture of openness with both staff and parents.

There are different strands to the safeguarding responsibilities:

The manager's responsibilities

- Has completed safer recruitment training
- Has completed designated person safeguarding training
- Maintaining the single central record and carrying out DBS checks
- Clear on their responsibilities in relation to safeguarding and prevent
- Has in place the necessary paperwork for monitoring and recording relating to safeguarding
- Ensuring staff are aware of, understand and are up to date on their safeguarding knowledge and responsibilities
- Monitoring children's attendance
- Keeping core training up to date and that all new staff are First Aid trained
- Ensure clear personal care policies are in place
- Consider how to avoid lone working and, if it is unavoidable, how this is managed
- Carrying out an annual staff suitability check
- Regularly remind parents to inform you if their contact details and emergency contact details needs updating

- Fire extinguishers and PAT testing.

The manager and staff suitability

This begins with your recruitment and selection process and the pre-employment checks completed including references, DBS, overseas checks if applicable, accounting for any employment gaps, right to work in the UK and understanding of the role ascertained through interview.

Your induction procedures and how new staff are supported and monitored. Ensuring they are made aware of your safeguarding policies and procedures including whistleblowing and their role in relation to the Prevent Duty.

It then continues with ongoing monitoring through supervision and appraisal processes and using strategies to ensure staff remain up to date and familiar with all safeguarding policies and procedures.

Staff also need to be made aware of the disqualification by association rule. If they are living with anyone who has been disqualified from working with children, they themselves are then disqualified.

The staff

- Registers, signing in and out
- Supervision at meal times and snack times
- Daily risk assessments
- Being aware of the whistleblowing policy and key safeguarding responsibilities
- Attending training.

The children

- Supporting children to manage risk in a variety of ways
- Having appropriate safeguarding policies and procedures in place
- Ensuring children have access to drinking water
- Begin to understand health and hygiene routines
- They are protected in extreme temperatures and sun cream is applied
- Dietary needs and allergies are catered for and managed safely e.g. with the use of placemats indicating dietary requirement.

The setting

- Clear fire escape plans and regular fire drills carried out, at different times of the day and on different days. It is important to carry them out at 'awkward' times as well, e.g. lunch
- Secure entry to the setting and secure grounds, policy for visitors
- Mobile phone, camera and smart watch policy
- Ensuring ratios are maintained at all times and appropriately qualified staff are employed
- Risk assessments in place and accident analysis completed to help minimise risk
- Insurance and registration documents displayed
- Evacuation safe place and lock down safe place
- Clear policies and strategies for behaviour management, with a member of staff having specific responsibility for behaviour.

Safeguarding responsibilities can seem daunting, but by ensuring and checking regularly everything is in place and that staff are confident about procedures, you can be more assured. This can be done in a variety of ways:

- Discussion in staff meetings
- Questioning individual staff
- Quizzes
- Use of case studies/scenarios, what would you do if...
- Flow charts and posters displayed with contact details.

Many local authorities offer safeguarding audits or have the paperwork available to download on their website so you can audit yourself.

As part of your broad safeguarding remit, do you have all of these in place if applicable:

- Single central record including DBS, qualifications, identity check
- Logs of any exclusions
- Logs of any incidents of discrimination including racist attacks
- Environmental health checks
- Risk assessments
- Policies and procedures file
- A list of referrals made to the designated person for safeguarding, with brief details of resolutions
- A list of all children who are an open case to social care/children's services and for whom there is a multi agency plan
- SEF (if used)
- Development plan/Quality Improvement Plan
- Records of conversation with local authority (if applicable)
- Qualifications and training record including First Aid and safeguarding
- Training matrix and records
- Pre-employment checklist
- Induction and professional development records for all staff
- Annual staff suitability check
- Complaints record
- Staff meeting minutes and agenda
- Accident record including accident forms and monthly accident analysis (it can be helpful as a prompt to include on the bottom of the accident form, a tick to identify if Ofsted and Riddor have been notified if necessary)
- Incident forms
- Pre-existing injury forms
- Medicine record (ensure you include time of the last dose given at home)
- Fire drill record (include time, day of week, date, time to evacuate, how many adults and how many children)
- Attendance record log of action taken for unexplained absence or frequent absences

- Registers, with a staff initial against the time the child arrives and the time the child leaves
- Staff register, including signing in and out for breaks
- Log of access to CCTV if applicable
- Display of named key carer and second key carer
- Log of checking contents of First Aid boxes/kits
- Lockdown policy
- Non-attendance tracking record.

What should be on the single central record?

- An identity check
- An enhanced DBS check
- Further checks on people living or working outside the UK (A police check needs to be obtained for anyone who has lived in a country other than the UK in the past 5 years.)
- A check of professional qualifications
- A check to establish the person's right to work in the UK.

Staff meeting discussion points

- Safeguarding/child protection scenario discussions.
- What does safeguarding mean?
- What are our different safeguarding responsibilities?

Case study Induction

Day Nursery Manager Lucy Meeson describes the induction process at her nursery.

On the first day I have a checklist which I go through and discuss with the member of staff, it covers anything and everything, including meeting the team, understanding everyone's role, policies and procedures, registers, overtime, pay, key carer role, holidays, supervision etc. We both sign and date, as I go through each point.

They are also assigned a mentor usually the room leader in their room, someone they go to with questions and anything they are unsure about.

During the first week, I meet with them everyday, then after 2 weeks and then after 3 weeks. The meetings are used to see how they are getting on and to clarify any issues and to raise any concerns. I also observe them in the middle of the first week and then a week or two later and feedback.

I aim to make the induction as supported as possible both for the benefit of the new practitioner and the nursery.

Lucy Meeson, Play Days Nursery, Wimbledon Hill

The signs of successful safeguarding arrangements

Indicators	Evidence in the setting	Action to improve
Children are protected and feel safe. Adults working with them know and understand the indicators that may suggest a child is suffering or is at risk at suffering abuse, neglect or harm and they take appropriate and necessary action in accordance with local procedures and statutory guidance.		
Leaders and managers have put in place effective child protection and staff behaviour policies that are well understood by everyone in the setting.		
Staff and other adults working within the setting are clear about procedures where they are concerned about the safety of a child and there is a named designated lead who is enabled to play an effective role in pursuing concerns and protecting children.		
Children can identify a trusted adult with whom they can communicate concerns. Children who are unable to share their concerns, e.g. babies and very young children, form strong attachments to those who care for them through effective implementation of the key person system.		
Written records are made in a timely way and held securely where adults working with young children are concerned about their safety or welfare. Those records are shared appropriately and, where necessary, with consent.		
Any child protection and/or safeguarding concerns are shared immediately with the local authority or relevant agency in the area where the concerned professional is working.		

Indicators	Evidence in the setting	Action to improve
There is a written plan in place that has clear and agreed procedures to protect a child. For children who are subject of a child in need plan or child protection plan or who are looked after, the plan identifies the help that the child should receive and the action to be taken if a professional working with the child has further concerns to report.		
Children who go missing from the setting they attend receive well-cordinated responses that reduce the harm or risk of harm to them. Providers are aware of how to implement the requirements of the Statutory Framework for the Early Years Foundation Stage when children go missing while in the care of the provider.		
Any risks associated with children misusing drugs, alcohol, self -harming, going missing, being vulnerable to radicalisation or being sexually exploited are known by adults who care for them and shared with the local authority children's social care service or other relevant agency.		
Children are protected and helped to keep themselves safe from bullying, homophobic behaviour, racism, sexism and other forms of discrimination. Any discriminatory behaviours are challenged and help and support are given to children about how to treat others with respect.		
Leaders in early years settings implement the required policies with regard to the safe use of mobile phones and cameras in settings.		
Leaders and staff make clear risk assessments and respond consistently to protect young babies and children while enabling them to take age-appropriate risks as part of their growth and development.		

Indicators	Evidence in the setting	Action to improve
Children feel secure and, where they may present risky behaviours, they experience positive support from staff. Babies and young children demonstrate emotional security through the attachments they form with those who look after them and through their physical and emotional well being. Staff respond with clear boundaries about what is safe and acceptable behaviour and they seek to understand the triggers for children's behaviour. They develop effective responses as a team and review those responses to assess their impact, taking into account the views and experiences of the child.		
Positive behaviour is promoted consistently.		
Staff and volunteers working with children are carefully selected and vetted according to statutory requirements. There is monitoring to prevent unsuitable people from being recruited and having the opportunity to harm children or place them at risk.		
There are clear and effective arrangements for staff development and training in respect of the protection and care of children. Staff and other adults receive regular supervision and support if they are working directly and regularly with children and learners whose safety and welfare are at risk.		
The physical environment for babies and children is safe and secure and protects them from harm or the risk of harm.		
All staff and carers have a copy of and understand the written procedures for managing allegations of harm to a child or learner. They know how to make a complaint and understand policies on whistleblowing and how to manage other concerns about the practice of adults in respect of the safety and protection of children.		

Adapted from 'Inspecting and Safeguarding in Early Years, Education and Skills Settings'. (Ofsted August 2016)

Safeguarding requirements for leaders and managers

Requirement	Evidence
■ Contributing to inter-agency collaboration in line with statutory guidance.	
■ Having due regard to the need to prevent people from being drawn into terrorism in accordance with the Counter-Terrorism and Security Act 2015.	
■ Carrying out reasonable checks, for example DBS checks, references.	
■ Ensuring that an effective child protection policy is in place, together with a staff behaviour policy, where applicable.	
■ Appointing a designated safeguarding lead.	
■ Prioritising the welfare of children and creating a culture where staff are confident to challenge senior leaders over any safeguarding concerns.	
■ Making sure that children are taught how to keep themselves safe.	
■ Putting in place appropriate safeguarding responses to children who go missing from early years and education settings, particularly on repeat occasions.	
Governing bodies, boards of trustees, registered providers, proprietors and management committees should prevent people who pose a risk of harm from working with children or learners by:	
■ Adhering to statutory responsibilities to check staff who work with children. (DBS, references).	
■ Taking proportionate decisions on whether to ask for checks beyond those that are required.	
■ Ensuring that volunteers are appropriately supervised.	
■ Ensuring that there are procedures in place to handle allegations against members of staff and volunteers.	
■ Making sure that there are procedures in place to handle allegations against other children.	

Adapted from 'Inspecting and Safeguarding in Early Years, Education and Skills Settings'. (Ofsted August 2016)

Inspecting arrangements for staff recruitment and vetting

Criteria	Evidence	Necessary actions
Ofsted expects early years providers to be able to demonstrate that they meet all regulations and duties for the purposes of the safeguarding judgement under leadership and management in the inspection handbook.		
Inspectors will check the single central record and they will check that the provider is able to produce evidence of suitability of relevant staff and adults to work with children...?	(DBS, qualifications, references).	
Inspectors should check the setting's policy and procedures for ensuring that visitors are suitably checked and monitored. (Students, volunteers etc).		
Registered early years providers are expected to make all records available at inspection. If evidence of suitability is not kept on-site, inspectors can accept this evidence later during the inspection, as long as it is provided before final feedback is given.		
For early years childcare inspectors should ascertain that the provider knows their legal obligation and has effective systems in place to find out information about whether a person many be disqualified.		
Where an early years setting has recruited volunteers who are not checked, inspectors should explore how the registered provider has reached this decision e.g. how it has assessed the level of supervision.		

Adapted from 'Inspecting and Safeguarding in Early Years, Education and Skills Settings'. (Ofsted August 2016)

Updating policies and procedures

Think about...	Yes/No	Comment/Action
Are there policies to meet all the requirements of the Statutory Framework of the EYFS?		
Does each policy fully reflect the setting's overall aims and objectives?		
Is each policy truly reflected in everyday practice?		
Does each policy have an overall statement of intent followed by the procedures of the setting that set out how they are fulfilled?		
Is regard for all the required and related legislation ensured and is it acknowledged and understood?		
Has a member of staff or a committee member been appointed to oversee the policy documents?		
Is there a regular slot on the agenda at staff meetings for addressing issues that may need revising in existing policy documents?		
Are all staff members involved when adopting new and revised policies?		
Do you regularly quiz the staff on policies either in practice or in meetings?		
Are policies made freely available for staff and parents to read?		
Are staff and if appropriate parents, given the opportunity to ask questions about policies?		
Are the policies written in a language that is clear, concise, easily understood and free from jargon and abbreviations?		
Are all policies reviewed annually or as often as necessary?		
Does each policy end with a declaration of adoption that is signed and dated by the setting manager, and a review date identified?		

References

Book and publications

Early Years Inspection Handbook (Ofsted September 2015)

Statutory Framework for Early Years Foundation Stage (DfE April 2017)

Inspecting Safeguarding in Early Years, Education and Skills Settings (Ofsted August 2016)

Progress Matters:Reviewing and Enhancing Young Children's Development (DCSF 2009)

The Functions of Management (DfES 2000)
Developing Management Skills (DfES 2000)

Rodd, J. *Leadership in Early Childhood* 2ndEd. (OUP 1998)

Langston, A and Smith, A *Managing Staff in Early Years Settings* (Routledge 1999)

Acknowledgements

Thank you so much to all the managers and Operations Directors who supplied their case studies: Zoe, Tracey, Linda, Caroline, Lucinda, Cassie, Lauren, Emma, Linda, Charline, Lucy, Sarah, Kerry and Becky.

Special thanks to Emma, Michelle and Stephanie, whom I haven't met but responded to me through social media.